M000289974

My Soul Longed for You

Michael + Melissa
May the Lord Bless you as
you read of Gods Amazing Love through
His Holy Spirit.   Edna Cassel

My Soul Longed for You

"AS THE DEER PANTS FOR THE WATER BROOKS,
SO PANTS MY SOUL FOR YOU, O GOD. MY SOUL
THIRSTS FOR GOD, FOR THE LIVING GOD"

PSALMS 42:2-3

EDNA CASSEL

Address all personal correspondence to:
Edna Cassel
Email: *cass4him@gmail.com*

Individuals and church groups may order books from the author directly, or from the publisher. Retailers and wholesalers should order from our distributors. Refer to the Deeper Revelation Books website for distribution information, as well as an online catalog of all our books.

Published by:
Deeper Revelation Books
Revealing "the deep things of God" (1 Cor. 2:10)
P.O. Box 4260
Cleveland, TN 37320
423-478-2843
Website: *www.deeperrevelationbooks.org*
Email: *info@deeperrevelationbooks.org*

Deeper Revelation Books assists Christian authors in publishing and distributing their books. Final responsibility for design, content, veracity and factuality of stories and statements, permissions, editorial accuracy, and doctrinal views, either expressed or implied, belongs to the author.

Contents

Dedication

I dedicate "My Soul Longed for You" to my sweet daughters, Kelsey Stoltzfus and Kendra Cassel, that the Lord will bless them as they grow in love for Him and His love for them. May they be the women of God He has called them to be.

With much love,
Mom

With Thanks...

I would like to express my sincere gratitude to the following individuals for their help and encouragement in making this book a reality...

- Brother Gerald Derstine for encouraging Phil and me spiritually and for writing the Foreword.
- My dad and mom for encouraging, then insisting that I write my story.
- My daughter Kelsey Cassel Stoltzfus for saying, "Mom you will probably write a second book after this one." That was a huge encouragement that she thought not only has God given me the strength to write one book, but if He asked me to do this, I would be able to do it again.
- My daughter, Kendra Cassel for being patient, understanding, and supportive during those long hours, helping me to spell words and just waiting for me to be there for her.
- My sweet Philip for all the times he prayed with me about the book, listened as I read to him, and gave his input.

Most of all, I want to thank the Holy Spirit for directing me each step of the way through the writing process. He is truly my helper. Thank You!

Foreword

Edna Cassel, the author of *My Soul Longed for You*, paints a very clear spiritual journey in this most interesting book of her quest to know God in a personal way. Some people may not have an interest in connecting with God, while others sincerely wish, even long, to know God in an intimate way.

Edna is very transparent in allowing both her positive and negative life encounters to express her deep, longing search for God. Readers who have come from a traditional and religious church culture will identify with the emotional family encounters she portrays and writes about in this book.

Being a close friend and spiritual mentor to both Edna and her husband Phillip, I admire their courage, boldness, and faith. I have watched them grow in the faith and grace of God over the years, and I know the reader will be greatly challenged to know in a more intimate way.

Christian are called by God to fulfill their purpose for living in this present world. The story in this book will help you connect where perhaps you may have lost your passion and lost your pursuit of God. I recommend that the readers search their inner lifestyle motivations as to what destination they expect to revere as a legacy.

My Soul Longed for You is an autobiography of Edna Cassel. I dare say it may be only the beginning of a very adventuresome journey for all the Cassel family. This story is so interesting, you will not be able to put the book down until the last page is read. The author has interspersed many Biblical verses representing the various experiences she encounters.

Be greatly blessed by the contents of this book and share this book with your friends. God bless your spiritual endeavors for God's glory.

Gerald G. Derstine, D.D.

President, Strawberry Lake Christian Retreat
Director, Founder, Israel Affairs, International
Chairman of the Board, Emeritus, Gospel Crusade, Inc.
Director, Founder, Institute of Ministry School

Introduction

There was a knock at the back door. When Phil answered it, I heard him say, "Jesse!" We had not seen my brother for several months. The two-and-a-half hour drive to our house was an outing not often taken. Jay and Nellene were in the kitchen getting ready to take the girls to Kendra's T-ball game. It was a warm spring Sunday afternoon, and I was happy to see my sibling.

"Come on girls! Let's go!" Nellene said to Kelsey and Kendra.
"Kendra, do you have everything you need for T-ball game?"
"I think so," Kendra responded with all smiles and eyes sparkling in her green T-ball outfit.

Jesse came in the living room with a stern look of concern on his face and said, "I know you do not want any visitors."

I walked over to him, hugged him, and said, "This is a surprise!"
"Yeah, I wanted to see you," he replied as he stepped back to take a look at me. "Dad and Mom tell me you are not doing so good. I wanted to come see you for myself." Jesse sat down with me on the sofa as his eyes, wide with concern, were watching every move I made.

"Edna, I always thought you were the strong one in the family!"

Those words came out of his mouth like an arrow to my soul and made me question myself. All I could say was, "I guess I'm not this time!" I don't think Jesse understood any better than I why I was so sick. My soul was sick, and answers were not something I possessed. Instead of answers to questions, my mind was in a whirlwind of confusion.

Jesse remembered the little sister who always tried to be there for all the family members when they needed an encouraging word or advice. He remembered the times when I would listen to his heart or help Grammy when she was so sick with cancer, or when I was just a listening ear for Wendy. I was always ready to help the family whenever I was needed.

I did not feel strong that day, because earlier that morning I had suffered another panic attack. When it gripped me, Phil was holding my left hand and Jay was holding my right hand while trying to usher me to a place of calmness and praying for the attack to stop. When I faced those bouts of overwhelming mental pressure, intense fear would grip me like Satan himself was perched on top of me.

As I went through the hyperventilating along with shaking and pain in my chest, I cried out to God, praying, "Please take this from me. I can't do this anymore!" I would think, *Lord, how did I get so sick? Help me! I don't know how to give it to You. I don't know how to place this fear and pain of the past at the foot of the cross. Show me, Lord! Please show me! I can't do this anymore! How did I get like this?"*

dad. The pregnancy did not go well. Mom and I were in danger of dying. Mom lost enough blood to have lost a baby, but I was born March 15, 1972.

When I was born, Mom said, "Genunk!" which means "Enough!" in Dutch. My mother named me *Edna Marie*, after Edna Detwiler and her sister, Marie. They are the ones who planted a seed in Mom's life for us to become Mennonites after Mom accepted Christ.

Growing up in the Mennonite church was much different than what most children experience. We did not do worldly things, so we would not go anywhere the world would go. We kept ourselves set apart from the world. We did not look like the world, either. My mother wore her covering and cape dress, and Dad wore a plain suit to church on Sundays. Even though we were more conservative Mennonites, my dad still had a problem with his anger. Being Mennonite does not take care of that! Only Christ can do that!

It was a dark night as I looked out the dining room window. Seeing the headlights of my Poppop and Grammy's car drive in the driveway, I ran as fast as I could to the back door. As Poppop entered the house, he scooped me up in his arms. Excitedly, I called out his name, as he asked, "Where is my baby kiss?" As I gave him a peck on his cheek, he said, "Where is my medium kiss?" As I gave a little bit bigger kiss on his cheek, he said, "Where is my big kiss?" Then I planted one of the biggest smackers of a kiss that I possibly could on his cheek.

My Poppop and Grammy did not look like us or anyone else who went to church with us. Poppop was shorter and combed his hair back to cover some gray hair. He wore glasses and always had a smile for me. I just knew I was special to him. Others would say he had a temper, but I never saw it, and he never got mad at me. My grandmother, with short, curly silver hair, had a voice everyone would remember. There were times we would go to a restaurant to eat as a family, and people there would hear Grammy talking from several tables away and know that Beatrice Gross was there. No one had a voice like my grandmother!

When I was five, my Poppop died, and my grandmother came to live in an apartment that was made for her in the garage built on the side of our house.

Being the youngest child, there were times when I felt like anything I had to say was not important. Many times at the supper table, I wanted to tell about my day like everyone else, but if I did not jump in and start talking at the right time, I wouldn't get to say a thing. Mom would whisper, "Honey, wait till they are done talking." So I would wait.

Then, when I started to talk, Dad would not hear me and would start talking. Since I was a stubborn child, I would keep talking at the same time. Dad would get mad, tell me to stop interrupting, and then I was sent to my room without supper for interrupting.

You would think that after not being able to eat supper many, many times, I would have learned. I spent a lot of time in my room or in the woods. The forest was my playground, and I could spend hours there with my cat and my imagination. Many nights, I would climb out of my bed and sneak over to Grammy's apartment and get in bed with her and watch TV. I wondered why God allowed Grammy to have a TV and not us? We didn't have a TV because Mennonites don't watch what the world does. That would be sinful. My grandmother went to an independent Bible church; she did not look or act Mennonite. It was hard to understand as a young girl why Grammy could do things we couldn't when I knew she read her Bible every morning. I would be watching television shows with Grammy, and Mom would come over and say, "Edna, get back to bed!"

Oh nuts, I got caught! I would think. I remember spending a lot of time with my grandmother. She eventually remarried and moved out. Later on in life, I helped her for several years when she was suffering with cancer.

When I was eight, we were at my great aunt and uncle's house for the weekend in Potter County, Pennsylvania. It was a hot day in July, and we had decided to go swimming in their pond. My brother, Jesse, my cousin, and one of their friends were swimming at one end of the pond, and I was at the other. I remembered seeing my sister do a handstand in the swimming pool earlier that summer and decided I could do it, too. The pond was pretty deep in the middle, but I planned to stay close to the edge. As I went under, holding my breath, I got my hands down to the bottom where it was very muddy and slimy and tried to bring my feet straight up to do the handstand.

I did it! I did it! I thought to myself. The only problem was, once I got my feet in the air, I could not figure out how to get back to a standing position. I struggled for a long time until, finally, my second cousin jumped in the pond and pulled me out.

"Are you Okay?" she asked. I started laughing to prevent myself from crying. The boys had no idea what had just happened. I thank the Lord my cousin was walking down the field to the pond just at that moment.

As a young girl, I would often hear fighting, and, at times, it seemed that there was no way of getting away from it except to go into my own little world and imagine things to be different than they were. Dad and Jesse did not get along at all. They would fight often, as they both suffered from a bad temper. There were times the tension was so thick in the house that you could, as they say, "cut it with a knife." I really did not know Jesse well as a child since he mostly stayed by himself or with his friends. Oftentimes, when dad was angry about something, Jesse would run off somewhere. He never wanted to be around until the fight was over.

Dad and Mom fought a lot, too. I cannot really call it fighting since Mom did not say much, but Dad would yell and let us all know that he was head of the home. (With Mennonites, the men are the heads of the home, and the women must listen to them and obey no matter how tough that is to do.) The children would be in trouble often; however, I never knew why I was in trouble. I was told it was because I hurt my dad's feelings. He was always very hurt and angry, which caused a lot of hurt in our family.

Consequently, as a small child, I lived with a great deal of fear, wondering when Dad would blow up, or when I would get my next spanking. Dad would take off his belt and spank my bottom, over and over again, while laughing. As a small child I thought that he must get enjoyment out of hitting us; I really did not think he loved me at all. As I got older, I realized he was not laughing out of enjoyment from hitting us, but purely out of nervousness.

I would sit behind my bedroom door when Dad came home from work at night just to listen to the tone in his voice to figure out if I wanted to come out or not. I was testing the temperature, so to speak, to determine his mood. You can learn a great deal about how people are feeling by the tone in their voices. I was afraid all the time. I bit my nails and would consistently dream of a different life. I think that is why I enjoyed the woods so much; it was a peaceful place of solitude where I was free to dream of any life I wanted. I did not know how to handle the pain of being so fearful, so I would not deal with it. It just became a part of me.

I started to be afraid of men in general, from school teachers to music teachers to men in the church. As a result of my ongoing fear, I cried a lot as a young child. Every morning, I would cry because nothing seemed right, and I did not have much joy. I could cry in the morning, because Dad was gone to work, but, at night, he did not want to hear crying.

"Stop that crying!" he would demand. "That is nothing to cry about."

I remember vividly one morning when I was in about the second grade. I was crying as my mom braided my long blond hair. Two braids was the typical way for little Mennonite girls to wear their hair. My brother's friend, Vernon, came walking in the back door, and instantly I stopped crying. Vernon was about 15 years old, and I just loved it when he was around. He was so funny, and when he came over Jesse was not as mean. I thought Vernon was the best person I knew. There was a presence about him that helped me feel peaceful. He would often walk over through the woods, and then he and Jesse would walk to school together. It broke all of our hearts when Vernon died a few years later. He drowned in Canada on a voluntary service mission's trip.

Even though we were more conservative Mennonites, my dad loved bluegrass gospel music, so he always wanted a child who could play the banjo. At age ten, I got a banjo, was taking lessons and doing pretty well with it. One day, at my music lesson, I had to go to the bathroom so badly, but since my music teacher was a man, I was too afraid to ask him if I could go. As a result, I had to pay the consequences of wetting myself and then being so embarrassed.

Going to church was always interesting; I had to sit very

quietly. My mom would not allow me to look at the Sears catalog all week, but when Sunday rolled around, she would bring it to church so I could look at it. This kept me quiet. I loved the toy section and the pictures. I remember many times being taken outside for a spanking for not sitting still. My mom would always take me out for the spankings at church, *but why does Dad do all the spanking at home?* I wondered.

I would find it interesting to see people sitting at the same place each week as if it was their very own bench. The women wore their hair up and wore a white covering. *They look like fish nets*, I thought. I stared at the hairstyles, and if any of the ladies had made a new dress, I would fix my eyes on the color of it, as color was always very important to me. During church I would draw a lot and dream of being able to paint a beautiful picture. The men wore dark-colored plain suits, and I would notice them giving each other a kiss on the cheek. "Mom, why do the men kiss each other?" I asked.

"That is a holy kiss," she replied, but I did not understand what that meant.

After one of the services when I was playing with my friends and they started to leave, Mom and Dad were still talking. I tried to be patient, but this time seemed like forever to me. I approached my mom while she was talking to Wayne Martin, a tall song leader with white hair who always wore a dark-colored plain suit. "Mom, I'm bored!" I said.

Wayne looked at me with a stern face, and in his deep voice said, "Edna, it is a sin to be bored."

If that is a sin, then I'm going to hell! As an active child, I would have rather been doing something instead of just sitting and waiting. Most of the time, the mere act of just sitting and waiting at church and at school with no interaction was the cause of my boredom, but I just got quiet and waited patiently.

 # Set Apart

For the Lord does not see as man sees; for men look at the outward appearance, but the Lord looks at the heart (1 Sam. 16:7).

One Sunday morning at church, an announcement was made that my closest friends, Karl and Kendall Keller, were going to be baptized and join the church. We were together at church, at school, and on the playground. To this day, we are still close friends. They are my brothers! When we got home from church, I asked my mom if I could talk to her in my room. Sitting on my bed with tears running down my cheek, I said, "Mom, I want to be baptized like Karl and Kendall." I knew in my heart that without getting baptized, I would go to hell when I died.

Dad walked in the room. "What's all the crying about?" he asked.

"Edna wants to be baptized," Mom answered.

"That's nothing to cry about," said Dad, but I could not stop crying, because I knew I was in big trouble and would be going to hell if I did not get baptized.

I was now eleven years old and joining the church. Since our pastor and his wife knew that their young daughter looked up to me, it seemed important to them and to my parents that I go to Lancaster County to the covering shop to help me find a head covering. Before we left for Lancaster, my sister Wendy helped me put my hair up the way she wore hers. When we got to the covering shop, one of the largest coverings was picked out for me. I was not happy about this at all, but since I knew it was expected of me, it made no sense to question it.

The next thing I knew, I was taking instruction class and learning all the things I could not do that were considered worldly sins. We were not to go where the world goes, and we were to distance ourselves from those in the world to avoid being influenced by them. We could not go to public places like bowling allies, fairs, skating rinks, and so forth. Later, I realized we needed contact with the world in order to influence others. We had the answer to all their questions: Jesus Christ!

I found out quickly that it was very important to look like you were a Christian so others would look at you and know that you were set apart. One Sunday night after church, we were sitting at the kitchen table, and Jesse walked in looking mad. He went on to say that the elders of the church took him aside and told him he had to shave his mustache, because he was not to have any facial hair. Jesse was angry, and I was confused. That just created more questions for me, because I did not understand. My thoughts were racing. *Every picture I had ever seen of Jesus showed Him with a beard, but Jesse can't have a mustache because it is a sin?* I inwardly questioned.

Before I realized it, on Sundays I was wearing my hair up with a covering on and a cape dress that someone was gracious enough to give my mom for me to wear. At eleven years of age, this was not what I called *fun*. I just did not want to go to hell, but all of this extra stuff was too much at times. I struggled with my hair, putting it up in a bun every day, trying to get it to look right with the covering. Because my hair was so straight, I knew it did not look as nice as Wendy's did with a natural wave. Dad thought so, too. I would struggle with the fact of not being pretty enough. At times, Dad would ask, "Why does your hair not look as good as Wendy's?" I did not have an answer for him.

One Sunday evening, my parents had guests over for supper. This would usually be a pleasant time, because Dad would be on his best behavior, and all would be well. This night, Mom made a wonderful meal, and the dining room table was made larger for the extra guests. As everyone was enjoying dinner and talking, Dad started telling our guests that Wendy was his favorite daughter because she reminded him of his wife, Pat. The guest got quiet, and the silence was so thick that you could "cut it with a knife," so to speak. I looked over at Jesse and tried not to cry. *Don't cry, Edna!* I told myself. *You have heard this before; don't cry, because Dad doesn't like it when you cry.* The thoughts where flooding my brain as I remembered Dad asking me why I wasn't as pretty as Wendy and wondering what I could do to please him. *When would I be good enough, or look the way he wanted me to look?*

Has the Lord done something in your life that you so thankful for because He looked at your heart when others may have been looking at what they thought they saw on the outside?

My Soul Longed for You

CHAPTER 3

My First Job

To everything there is a season, a time for every purpose under heaven (Ecc. 3:1).

A lot of changes took place when I was twelve. The best part was that Dad took Christian counseling with Mom, and he was not physically abusive any more. We left the Haycock Mennonite church where I had joined just the year before. When you get baptized in our church, you also join the church as if one has something to do with the other. Dad said that the church was getting to be too legalistic, so we moved on.

I also started attending a new school; I had been going to the Mennonite school, which was hard for me at times. It was an ACE school, which allowed you to work at your own pace but did not offer much interaction with other students. This system was not good for me since it did not keep me motivated. I would stare out the window, daydreaming and drawing. In fact, I did some of my best drawings during school time. Passing notes to Karl was a real joy, too, or playing Tic-tac-toe. Sitting in our own little cubicles with dividers, we were left alone completely to do school work. In order to pass notes to Karl, I would slip the piece of paper under my divider and over to his side.

The new school I went to was a Christian school with a traditional school setup. The classroom had about twenty students and a teacher. Leaving LaHay, the little Mennonite school, to go to Plumstead Christian held me back a year because of poor grades in math and English. This school had about 300 children from sixth to twelfth grade; however, the school I came from had about twenty-five students in the entire school. Plumstead Christian was a very new experience for me, and I was the only one in the school who wore a head covering.

Edna Cassel age 14

Are these people Christians if they don't wear the head covering? I wondered. The women have shorter haircuts, and they can even wear pants on field trips. I convinced my parents to let me wear the black veil to school; it seemed more stylish than the typical white covering that most of the conservative Mennonites wore.

I was very insecure and shy at this new school, but I had been outgoing at the old school. Now, people laughed at me regularly, asking me questions about why I wore the covering. I did not have a good answer for them because my answer didn't even make sense to me. By the time I was thirteen, I looked thirty. My glasses were too small for my face, and because we were poor, we could not afford to get bigger ones. I wore my hair up in a veil, and I wore hand-me-down clothes that were all out of style. Still, I made a few good friends, but they all lived forty-five minutes to an hour away.

On my first day at Plumstead, I walked in the class, met my teacher and sat down. I was so nervous; no one looked like me. I wore my brown plaid dress with a mock corduroy vest; I had my hair up in a bun; and my veiling was in place. I looked around my class and thought to myself, *Oh my goodness, I am the tallest girl in the whole class!* All the other girls were so short compared to me. Not only did I stick out because I looked different, but I was also a foot taller than the other students. I sank down in my chair and did not sit straight. After the first class, another new girl walked over to me and asked, "Whose mother are you?" with a tone in her voice like, *Why are you still here? Why didn't you drop your kid off and go home?*

"I am not a mother," I replied. "This is my first day of school here." I was mortified. No wonder the kids looked at me funny. They didn't even think I was a student.

After being at school a few weeks, one of the students came up to me and asked, "What country are you from?"

With complete confusion, I asked why she would ask that. "I have lived here my whole life," I informed her.

"Why do you talk so funny?" she asked. It wasn't until I was older that I realized I spoke English with a lot of Dutch words included, so people did not understand me at times.

I remember some of the teachers telling me that I must be

a good influence for the rest of the children. I was expected to act differently than the rest of my peers because of how I looked. I would come home from school, go to my room and sleep. Often I would lie in bed and daydream. This was my way to a life I could only dream of. Today I realize *that* can get dangerous, depending on where you let your thoughts and dreams take you!

When I turned fourteen, Dad and Mom said I needed to get an after-school job, but I was so scared to do this. Mom went with me when I applied to the Quakertown Community Home, a retirement home. I got the job cleaning the supper dishes and the dining room. I enjoyed my job. After a short time, I realized I would rather work there than anywhere else. I learned a lot from my boss, Darlene Cross, who taught me how to be organized and how to clean and cook. I worked there off and on for thirteen years. Darlene and her husband, Roger, were a very good influence on me. I enjoyed watching them interact with their children. Roger would take his daughter out on dates or prepare her favorite meal just so they could sit down and have time together. I often thought that he must be the best dad I knew.

My dad and a friend of his started a home church. It was going well for Dad, and he enjoyed being able to teach and preach, but I felt like we were playing church because it wasn't in a regular church setting. I started to get very rebellious. When I went out with friends, I would take off my dress and head covering and let my long hair hang down. I would be gone as much as I could, because fun became the main thing for me.

My mom realized it was important for me to be involved in a regular youth group. Karl and Kendall would sometimes come to home church, and another friend would attend, but it wasn't like we had the type of youth group that my sister and brother had growing up. So, we visited other Mennonite churches for a few months.

We settled at Finland Mennonite Church because a lot of young people went there, and my parents liked Pastor Steve Landis. By this time, I was fifteen and enjoyed doing things with others my age. I became a very big social bug since I was so shy and timid at school. My first youth social was pizza and bowling. This was a switch considering I was taught to stay away from the bowling alleys where the world attended! I eventually realized that the Mennonite church you went to determined what was a sin by the way you looked. There were a lot of young guys in the youth group there, and one of them in particular kept smiling at me every time I glanced his way. "What's this guy's problem?" I asked the girl who invited me.

"Oh, that's Phil Cassel. He's like that all the time. He likes to smile at the girls," she explained. She told me he was strange, so I never thought too much more about it after that. He was always around, never saying anything, just listening and smiling at me.

How do you deal with change and new seasons in your life? Do you look at this as adventure that the Lord is taking you through, or do you dread it, wishing things would stay the same?

With each new season, if we allow God to work in each of us, there will be growth and we will become stronger with each new task. Some changes will come that can be enjoyable and others you may dread worse than having teeth pulled, but God will never leave you or forsake you. Ask Him to hold you and carry you through.

CHAPTER 4

The Accident

But He was wounded for our transgressions, He was bruised for our iniquities, the chastisement for our peace was upon Him. And by His stripes we are healed (Isa. 53:5).

We had been going to Finland Mennonite Church for nine months. I was sixteen, driving, working, and going to school. Karl and Kendall came with their family to this same church after we did, so we were always together. One weekend at a MYF (youth) retreat, I got to know one of the guys in the youth group better, and a few weeks later, he asked me out on a date. I was so excited. I enjoyed every part of having someone think I was so special. We did so much together over the next few weeks.

One day, December 29, 1988, to be exact, I picked Kendal and another girlfriend up, and off we went to Pizza Hut. We had the day off from school, so we met my boyfriend and went out for lunch. Christmas break was wonderful, having the time off from school, so we decided to go for lunch since I had to work that evening. We had such a great time, you know the way teenagers are when they are with their friends!

We dropped my boyfriend and girlfriend off, and as Kendall and I were driving to his house, he was so funny, as always. He was digging makeup out of my purse and trying it on to make me laugh. Since I was not going to the conservative church at this time, I was wearing my hair down and only wearing my head covering on Sundays, so wearing makeup just seemed like the thing to do.

After dropping Kendall off, I was driving back home and needed to be at work by 4:30. The last thing I remember was turning on Route 663. I woke up a week later in the shock trauma unit at Lehigh Valley Medical Center, pulling a hose out of my nose. I heard the nurse say to the orderly, "Do you want to trade patients? She will not stop pulling her hose out; this is the third time today." There were machines, hoses, and wires all over me.

"You're awake! I will call for your parents," the nurse said to me. She called my parents, and I have never seen my mom look so badly.

"Mom, are you okay? You look horrible," I said.

"We have been through a lot this past week," Mom replied. Then, she and Dad went on telling me that a drunk driver hit me, and I had been in a coma for a week. When the hospital staff removed the respirator and turned off the ventilator, I was moved to the intensive care unit. Our pastor, Steve Landis, came to see me, and I told him, "I am going home on Wednesday," which would only be a week away.

"No, the doctors said you would be here for about two months," he replied.

"No, I am going home Wednesday," I reiterated.

My heart was bruised, because the steering wheel was literally bent in half from the impact of it into my chest. My right leg had been smashed under the engine of my car. I had surgery to rebuild my right ankle, and a cast was put on while I was in a coma. The doctors put a plate, two screws, and seven pins in my ankle. I had plastic surgery on my face, as the right side of my face was scraped like someone took a cheese grater to it. There were eighty stitches in my cheek alone. The doctors took skin from behind my right ear to graft above my right eye to make a new eyelid for me. My scalp was ripped back on the left side of my forehead into my hairline. My right hand was smashed, and my pointer and middle fingers were badly smashed and in a cast. There was a tube coming out of my right knee, and my knee was cut down to the bone but not through it.

The doctors told my parents that where my scalp was ripped, my brain was bruised, where my soul is! We did not understand what the doctor meant, so Dad asked, "What do you mean where Edna's soul is?"

The doctor replied, "That's the part of her brain that makes her who she is, her personality."

Tuesday came, and the doctor said, "Edna, would you like to go home tomorrow?"

"I knew I was going home tomorrow!" I confidently replied.

While I was in a coma, I had a 50/50 chance of making it. I had been in a coma for several days with no sign of improvement. My dad continued to pray to God for mercy. "Please have mercy on us!" Dad also asked our pastor at Finland Mennonite if he would anoint me with oil for healing like the Bible talks about in James 5:14-15: "Is any one among you sick? Let him call for the elders of the church, and let them pray over him, anointing him with oil in the name of the Lord. And the prayer of faith will save the sick, and the Lord will raise him up." Verse 16 says, "Confess your trespasses to one another, and pray for one another, that you may be healed."

After the elders of the church, the pastor, and my parents

anointed me with oil, they went down to the chapel in the hospital and confessed sins and asked the Lord's forgiveness, praying for one another, which is very important when asking the Lord to heal you. Within five minutes of being anointed with oil, I started coming out of the coma.

While I had been driving down the two-lane highway prior to my accident, the drunk driver crossed over the cement median strip and into my lane. I went to the outside lane to avoid being hit, but the driver kept driving toward me. He came directly at me and as his truck struck mine, he literally drove up on the hood of my brown Dodge Aries. His red pick-up truck then flipped over so that it was laying with tires up as my car continued to spin in circles a few times until it stopped. There was blood everywhere, including running down my face, and glass was smashed all around me.

Edna's car after the accident

The drunk driver came over to my window and pulled on me. He knew enough in his drunken state that I needed to get out. Because I was so smashed in the car and the engine was on my right leg, there was no way he could ever pull me out. Some people who had been driving by stopped to help. "Stop! Stop pulling at her! You will not get her out," they exclaimed.

The drunk driver would not listen, so one of the men just punched him right in the nose, which started to bleed. This was the only injury the drunk driver had from the accident.

When the police and the ambulance got to the scene of the accident, they checked my pulse, and I had none. They thought I was dead until I started to scream, and then there was a mad rush to get me out of the car. I was alive, but I was trapped for over an hour, and the Jaws of Life had to cut me out. Because of all the blood I had lost and since it was freezing outside, I also had hypothermia. I was flown by helicopter to Lehigh Valley Medical Center.

Mom would not let me look in a mirror for a couple of weeks. She said that I had a fit when I had a pimple, so she certainly did not want me to see the way my face looked after the accident. After two weeks, I finally convinced her to let me see my face. When I looked in the mirror, I asked, "Where is my eyebrow?"

"The plastic surgeon does not think it will grow back because of the skin graft that was needed to make your new eyelid," Dad explained. "You may want to get an eyebrow pencil and pencil it in at some point."

"Do you want me to get a turban and wear that, too?" I asked. I was not accepting at all the thought of wearing fake eyebrows. I had many doctors appointments the next few months. When I went to the plastic surgeon for a check-up to see about the next step for follow-up surgery, he walked in and said, "Edna, you have an eyebrow!"

"Of course I have an eyebrow," I replied. I did not expect anything less than being normal again. I had several months of therapy to learn how to walk again. It was painful. People were praying for me all over, including other states, and many of them I did not even know. Everyone called me "the miracle girl."

> *Who Himself bore our sins in His own body on the tree, that we, having died to sins, might live for righteousness, by whose stripes you where healed (1 Peter 2:24).*

> *Jesus Christ the same yesterday, and today and for ever (Heb. 13:8).*

He paid the price on the cross for our sins, our sickness, and our infirmities. He can heal you of a physical, emotional, or spiritual need. Is there something you are dealing with now that you need to ask the Lord to heal you in Jesus' name to make you whole again?

> *Father, in Jesus' name, I come to You right now asking You to cover my spirit, soul and body with the blood of Jesus Christ. I ask that You would reveal anything in me that may be causing this infirmity, and I ask in Jesus' name that You would take it to the foot of the cross so that I will not hold on to it any longer. I give it to You, Father! Thank You, precious Jesus! Amen.*

CHAPTER 5

Waiting on the Lord

But those who wait on the Lord shall renew their strength, they shall mount up with wings like eagles, they shall run and not be weary, they shall walk and not faint. (Isa. 40:31).

At times, it felt like the days were so long even though God had dramatically saved me from death and I was healing much better than the doctors expected. Everything took longer with one good leg and one good hand. I was used to using my right hand, but it did not take too much to switch over to the left and be able to write.

Besides the therapy and having tutors keep me up to where I should be in school, I also went to a support group for patients who had been in the shock trauma unit or in a coma. We were told by the doctors that I would never remember what had happened to me and that it was my body's way of protecting me from the trauma that had happened. I was also told that none of us who were in the shock trauma unit would remember what that unit looked like. "I know what it looks like," I said.

"That's not possible," I was told.

"Well, I do!" Then, I went on to describe it. "There is a desk in the middle of the room and beds are all around the outside walls with only curtains dividing each area where the patients' beds are."

"How do you know that?" I was asked.

"That's exactly what it looks like! I saw it when Vernon came to see me," I explained. (Vernon was my brother's friend who would come over to my house in the morning before going to school, which I loved so much. Later, he drowned in a lake.)

There were other things I could recall when I was in a coma. I remember my sister talking to me about meeting my boyfriend at the time. I knew he was there in the trauma unit room when she was speaking. Even though I did not see anyone, I knew they were there at certain times; it was as if I could sense their presence with me.

When I came out of the coma, I also told my parents that the patient in the bed next to me had slit his throat. They went to the nurse to ask if that was the case, and she confirmed that it was true. She also told my parents that I was the only one in the shock trauma unit who had not been injured from self-infliction.

I remember there were times in therapy that were just so hard and hurt so badly that my eyes would well up with tears. The boyfriend I had at the time came and supported me every day for months. His grandfather was the most awesome man. He had a loving, supportive way about him and made me laugh. I liked being around him, as he often encouraged me. His name was Harold, and he had an accident shortly after I did, so he was with me in therapy. We would schedule our appointments at the sports medicine center at the same time. I remember one day when we were both getting our legs stretched at the same time, and as tears were running down my face, he said, "You can do it, Edna! You can do it!" I will never forget his support as I went through that. Sometimes, I think he had to go through what he did just so he could be there for me.

I was told that I would walk with a limp and may have to wear my air cast indefinitely while using a cane. Today I walk just as good as anyone, and without an air cast. I have been completely healed, and I have the scars to remind me of His healing power in my life.

By the time April came, I had just turned seventeen in March and was feeling like a show exhibit when people came by to visit. "People are just coming to see what I look like," I said to Mom. My attitude was not right, and I was feeling like I was stuck in a house with nothing to do apart from simply thinking about what I wished I could do. Thinking that people only wanted to see what this 'miracle girl' with a new face looked like, I suggested to my mom, "You could charge at the door when people come to visit." Then, I asked, "May I please go away for a while, anywhere, just some place different?" I felt like I really needed a change after four months of healing.

Mom and Dad called friends of theirs who lived in Bradford County, Pennsylvania, to see if I could stay with them for a while. By this time, I was walking with a limp, and I had the cast off my hand. My parents drove me up to Doug and Leona Graybill's house, the pastor and his wife of Canton Mennonite Church. During that time, Leona helped me through the break-up with my boyfriend, as she listened and gave advice. We became very close, and I did not know at the time that she and her husband would be such an influential part of my life in the future.

When I returned home from Doug and Leona's home, I started to think about doing something with my life. I figured that my life must have been spared for a reason, so I started looking into going on a mission's trip to Chili. I went back to school for just a short time, but could not stay focused long enough to stay all day. Plus, my leg would swell up from sitting with it hanging down all the time. I would see flashes of light, and my eyes would water when I read for too long. I could not handle being in the gymnasium for too long, especially when it was really noisy. My body was still in shock from the car accident. Since I had tutors right after the car accident, I convinced Mom and Dad that I should get tutors again to graduate. So Mom and I did this together. She had not gotten her high school diploma when she was young, so we got a tutor and took our GED. I graduated a year earlier than all my classmates, but it was right on time for me since I was held back in the sixth grade when I switched schools.

I was looking forward to the missions trip to Chili, but then it was canceled. I was so disappointed. I left my job at the Quakertown Community Home to work at Souderton Mennonite Nursing Home. I wanted to care for the elderly and not just clean their rooms and make their dinner, so I got certified as a nursing assistant.

Waiting can be a very difficult task! Waiting on the Lord can be hard at times, but He has the perfect timing for everything. Is there something you are waiting on the Lord for and you are not seeing the results as quickly as you would like? He knows what He is doing; He goes before you, and He goes behind you. He loves you, and you need to trust in His timing, no matter how hard.

CHAPTER 6

Missions Work in Mexico

For I know the thoughts that I think towards you, says the Lord, thoughts of peace and not evil, to give you a future and a hope (Jer. 29:11).

When I was eighteen, my dad said to me, "Edna, Phil Cassel is a nice guy. I think he is more your type than your other boyfriend. If you like him, you marry him!"

I had an attitude and an answer for just about everything. I did not like Phil. He smiled at me and watched me all the time. I would get teased in youth group that he was my little puppy. You could usually find Phil around me listening to every word I said. Some time went by and Dad said, "Edna, I think that tonight at Bible study, Phil is going to ask you out."

"I doubt it!" I replied.

"I have been observing him watch you, and I think he will ask you out tonight," Dad said. That night at Bible study, Phil followed me out to my car and said, "Edna, I want to ask you something. Would you go with me to my work Christmas dinner? We are going to Sight and Sound."

"I'll have to let you know," I said with hesitation in my voice. I then went over to a friend's house before heading home. I was so worked up that he would actually ask me out, because this was the same guy that when my girlfriends and I saw him pumping gas in town, we'd teasingly say, "There's Phil

Cassel, the man I am going to marry . . . NOT!"

When I got to my friend's house and told her Phil had asked me out, her sister who was older than us, said, "Edna, Phil helps me out at church with the Boys and Girls Club. He is a really nice guy. Why don't you give him a chance?" So, a few days later, I called him and told him I would go with him and that it sounded like fun.

As I got to know Phil, I saw a side of him that no one knew, a side I think was hidden as a gift just for me. I started liking him more and more. He did not talk much, but he liked to be with me, and he acted like a gentleman. As the months went on, I realized he had very low self-esteem, so I would encourage him as much as I could. We started dating in November 1990, and after a few months, he went on a missions trip with a bunch of guys from church to chop wood for the Indian school at Poplar Hill in Canada. He was gone for two weeks. During that time, I realized he was the guy I wanted to marry. I was getting tired of dating and was hoping for a secure commitment. About a week after Phil returned from Canada, he told me he wanted to marry me but probably not until another two years.

I was working full time as a nurse's aide and loved it. I took some time off to go on a ten-day missions trip to Mexico. I went with twelve other young people to help remodel a church there. I stayed with a doctor and his family. When the doctor realized I was a nurse's aide, he asked, "Will you come with me into the streets of Mexico City tomorrow and help me? I could use your help!"

"I would be glad to," I answered. Wow! What an awesome experience that was! We went into the dirtiest rundown places where people were too sick to get out of bed and had flies all over them. I helped the doctor with whatever I could, and I had the best day helping him. He asked if I would consider staying with him and his family because he was moving his family to the mountains of Mexico where there were no doctors to help with the sick. "I could use your help," he stated. Then, he asked me three more times that week. I wanted to stay so badly, but I also wanted to marry Phil. I decided that right away I would tell Phil what had happened and then see what he had to say about it.

When I returned home, Phil was at the airport waiting to pick me up. As we were driving , he said, "Edna, I do not ever want you to leave me again."

"Well, that is what we need to talk about," I replied. "I was asked to stay in Mexico, but I want to marry you, too."

Phil smiled at me and said, "Someday, we will do missions together."

The missions trip to Mexico was in April; Phil asked me to marry him July 1990, and we got married March 16, 1991, the day after my nineteenth birthday. We rented a small one-bedroom apartment at a very good price of $350 a month, but Phil believed that by renting we were throwing our money away. We lived in the apartment for nine months and then found a cheap house in Milford Square, Pennsylvania, a house that was once a carriage house turned into a two-bedroom home. It was a cute little house for a family just starting out. We celebrated our first anniversary there and found out that same week that we were going to have a baby. Phil got quite upset and did not want to talk about it, as if that was going to make it go away.

We had not planned on a child at this point, because we were planning on waiting five years before starting a family. We thought we would be financially better off by that time. On our anniversary trip to Lancaster County for the weekend, Phil barely spoke to me. He did not know how to handle the change, and he was thinking of how it would affect us financially.

I was upset, not because I was pregnant but because of how Phil was handling this. We were both young; I was 20, and Phil was 22. As we were sitting in complete silence at the restaurant, I told Phil I would be back, and that I need to go to the restroom. When I returned to the table and told Phil that I was bleeding and did not want to lose the baby, that did something to him. From that point on, he wanted our baby. I guess the thought of losing the baby scared him more than the thought of how we were going to support a child.

Phil and Edna on their wedding day

The pregnancy was hard. I was in bed for two weeks until the doctors were sure that the baby was fine. I was sick for five months with what most people call "morning sickness." I had about three hours in the afternoon that I was not sick. Then, on November 6,1992, Kelsey Lynn Cassel was born, and she was the most beautiful baby either of us had ever seen. Phil cried when she was born; he was so happy she was okay.

We lived in our house in Milford Square. Phil was working as a builder, and I was working at Quakertown Community again. I would work when Phil was home, so Kelsey would only stay at my mom's for a short time a couple times a week until Phil could come get her. On Sunday, we went to the church Phil grew up in, but something seemed to be missing. We visited other churches, but nothing fit. We traveled up to Bradford County to Doug and Leona Graybill's about twice a year since we liked the Mennonite church where Doug pastored. Often, we hated to return home after a weekend up there. I would say to Phil, "Maybe someday we could move up here."

"That's just a dream," he'd reply.

We were preparing for another child. Kelsey was getting to the point where she did not like to see friends leave with other children, so we decided that we would try for another child. I knew in my heart that would be it for us and children. Phil had said early on in our marriage that we would have only two children, and that is all we could afford. I did not complain even though I had hoped for more children. With Phil the head of the home, I figured that if he believed that was all we could afford, then two children it would be. Phil made many decisions regarding our finances, and just about everything decided upon was based on the money that was in the checking account. This was how it was expected to be done considering Phil was the primary provider.

Kendra Mae was born on June 8, 1995. She was a totally different personality than Kelsey, but we loved her all the same. She did not sleep through the night for many months and would get stomach aches and cry and cry. As she got older, she did not talk as soon as Kelsey, but one day I realized she did not need to talk, because Kelsey did all the talking for her.

After Kendra's birth, I got my tubes tied so we would not have any more children. We never prayed about that decision; we just knew it was what needed to be done if we were going to have a normal lifestyle and not live in debt. As the years went on, I suffered from many physical problems because of that decision. Getting my tubes tied put my body in shock and produced a faster growing rate of endometriosis, which I would suffer from for several years.

There have been times in our life that we tried to take direction into our own hands and not seek the Lord for His purpose and will for us. Phil and I have had to ask forgiveness for that and to learn to trust in the Lord, because He knows the purpose and plans He has for us.

Is there anything in your life that the Lord is telling you right now that He would like you to give to Him, and that He has a purpose for you in that situation?

CHAPTER 7

Depression

As the deer pants for the water brooks, so pants my soul for you, O God. My soul thirsts for God, for the living God. When shall I come and appear before God? My tears have been my food day and night (Ps. 42:1-3).

During the fall of 1996, we went on a weekend getaway to see Doug and Leona. As I was visiting with Leona, I told her how we never wanted to leave after our visit and that we often talked about living in Bradford County some day. She just smiled and said, "I often thought you would." Then, she told me about a builder who attended the Mennonite church who needed help. When we got home, I shared with Phil that there was a builder who needed extra help up in Canton.

He said, "We will put the house up for sale the beginning of the year, and if it sells, we will move up there." We had lived in Milford Square for five years. The house was sold, and we moved July 1, 1997. Phil got the job over the phone, and we bought a house on the hill across from Canton Lake. This was a big change moving away from all our friends and family in the area where we had grown up. Kelsey was now four, and Kendra had just turned two.

While we lived in Canton, we were very involved with the Canton Mennonite Church. The people there had become family to us, and when we needed anything, they were right there. I had several surgeries during our time in Canton, and dealing with endometriosis, the church family was there every time I needed help. When I had my leg in a cast, they were right there helping us. The people in this church became a very important part of our lives.

In 2001, I asked the board of the Christian day school if I could work there in exchange for the girls' schooling. Kelsey was in second grade, and Kendra was just ready to start kindergarten. A man who went to church with us who was also on the school board, said to me, "How about being our office manager?"

I did not know about doing this because my spelling was terrible, and, I had never worked in an office before. However, he seemed to think I could do it. He said that dealing with people was the most important thing when people called the school, and that because I was such a people-person, he thought I would be good at it. The job was okay at first, but the longer I worked in the office, the more I did not want to be there. I would pour all my energy into getting things done right at school, and then I did not have enough to give to my family.

I remember the night when I told Kendra and Kelsey to go and play because Mommy needed to lie down. I seemed to have to do this a lot after work because I was so tired. I would lie in our dark bedroom as the day was ending and while it was getting closer to Phil coming home from work.

Kendra came to the side of the bed and said, "Mommy! Mommy!" I could not answer her. I heard her, but it was like I was not there. I did not even have enough strength to say, "What do you want, Honey?"

She went on saying, "Mommy! Mommy, are you going to get up soon? I am hungry!" Before long, a very disappointed little girl left the room, still hungry, and wondering when she was going to get supper.

Phil worked a ten-hour day and was tired when he came home. For several weeks, he would just get the girls and himself something to eat. I would lie in bed in the dark, too tired, physically and emotionally, to move. Phil did not ask me if I was okay; he just did what needed to be done. There were times I really struggled with wondering if Phil even loved me. He would not ask me how I was feeling , and he would not give me words of encouragement. I thought to myself, *Am I good enough for him*? He would just mind his own business, do what he had to do, and go to work. Our marriage was wearing very thin!

Whenever anything big came up that we needed to decide together or talk about, Phil would often just get quiet, trying as hard as he could to ignore the situation, as if it would go away. He did not want to share his opinion or didn't have one to share. I really didn't know how hurt my husband was at the time. I just thought it was a cruel thing he was doing to me by not sharing his heart and not helping to make decisions, especially when it came to decisions about our girls. It seemed to me that the only thing that was important to Phil was his job and making money, and if he put in a full day's work and made money to pay the bills then I should not expect to have his opinion on other matters such as raising the children.

At times when the money was tight, Phil would get very quiet and not talk to me or have anything to do with me intimately, as if it was all my fault. I took this personally and felt like I was being blamed for something that was not my fault. I remember when other women I knew were buying clothes and all kinds of things for their homes, but I would not. I hated going grocery shopping, because Phil would ask me how much I spent, and then he would get very moody and snappy or would not talk to me. I felt like I was in a battle that I could not win. I didn't know how to buy groceries for a family of four on $60 a week, but I started learning some shortcuts with the food, like freezing it and getting free bread from a friend who worked for a bread company.

When I was working at the school, the communication between Phil and me was so bad. My emotions just got worse, and I did not talk about how I felt. I had learned at a very young age not to show too much emotion, because it could make me cry. I had been told so many times to stop crying that I think it was ingrained in me not to cry.

The anger and hurt feelings were starting to make me feel numb, and I was starting not to care anymore. I developed a pattern of lying in my bed and not doing my housework or tending to my girls. I just went to the school and then came home to sleep. My soul was so sick, and I had no idea what to do about it. I should have had it all together as my life had been spared as a young girl; therefore, God must have had a purpose for me, but I was in bad shape. Although I got saved when I was young and went to church every Sunday, that was still not enough to heal my soul. And the worst part about it was, I had no idea how bad off I really was!

One day, when I was lying on my bed in the dark bedroom and wasn't feeling as badly as I had felt some other days, I got to thinking this situation just wasn't good or normal. It definitely was not fair to Kelsey and Kendra, so I called our pastor's wife, Leona. When Leona answered her phone, I said, "Leona, I need help! I don't know what is wrong with me, and I cannot do anything. I have no motivation. I come home from work, and all I do is sleep."

I am not sure what else I told her at that point, but the urgency in her voice made it clear to me that I was not okay. "I want you to hang up," she said. "I am going to call a counselor who has been using the church as an office a few days a week. I am going to make an appointment for you, and as soon as Phil gets home I want you to tell him to call me."

Phil came home a few minutes later, and I gave him Leona's message. I still do not know what Leona said to Phil, but I do know there was an urgency to get me help as soon as possible. Leona had made a appointment the very next day for me to see this counselor, and she asked Phil if he could take off work to be there also.

The heaviness was so bad, and I wondered if I was worth anything to anyone. I was never good enough for my dad. Was I good enough for Phil? Everything seemed to be my fault. I was supposed to be a good Mennonite woman and submit to my husband, but what do I submit to? I wondered. *He is not taking leadership of our home, so how do I submit to that?* I thought. *What am I going to do? I feel so numb! I do not have a desire for anything or to be around anyone. I always wanted to be a mother, and now I just want to be left alone. I just can't do this anymore.*

The next morning, Phil and I went to the little nursery in the back of the church where Leona, the counselor, Phil, and I were to meet for the counseling session. I seriously do not remember the questions the counselor asked me. All I know is that he only had to ask a few of them. My emotions were so raw that when he did ask, all the hurts, all the confusion, all of every part of everything I ever knew or believed spilled out on the carpet, and there was no running away from it now. I had stuffed and stuffed so much down into my heart to avoid dealing with the pain that when he began asking me questions, it was like a geyser exploded into the light that filled my whole being with utter despair.

The memories were flooding me from the past. They were

coming up at such a fast speed that I could not handle it. Here were all these things I had forgotten, so I would not have to feel. They kept coming, and the more they would surface, the more the counselor would ask questions. Phil was hearing things for the first time that he did not even know had happened to his wife. I started to cry and cried violently. I wept so loudly and so long that I did not know if I would ever stop.

"You need to get her hospitalized in a psychiatric ward. She needs to be evaluated," the counselor advised Phil. He then gave Phil some hospital suggestions. Phil was overwhelmed, and I knew it, but there was nothing I could do to help.

"We will help with the girls, and I will call Jay and Nellene and let them know," said Leona. Jay and Nellene were our Sunday school teachers at church, and a little before all of this happened, they befriended us like we were their second family. Their children lived in Lancaster, three and a half hours away, and our parents and family also lived that same distance away from us. They thought a lot of us and our girls, and Leona knew they would want to be there and help us in any way they could.

Once Phil got me back home, the memories kept flooding! During the counseling session, I remembered when I was eight years old I heard my dad fighting with my mom. I do not know what it was about, but dad was so angry at mom. I could hear the fighting. They were in the hall and had just come out of their bedroom. I was standing at the other end of the hall, and saw Dad yelling at Mom with his belt wrapped around her neck.

I cried, "Daddy, stop it! Daddy, stop it!" as he grabbed my mom's hair with one hand and had his other hand with the belt around her neck. He was yelling at her to obey him, and he pulled a hand full of hair out of her head and ripped her covering off her head.

I cried again, "Daddy, stop it! You are hurting Mommy," as I ran down the hall and jumped up at him and landed on his arm, trying to get his hands off Mom. I was so light that Dad just took his left arm I was hanging on and threw me down the hall. I literally flew through the air and hit the door jamb of the bathroom as my brother Jesse ran out of his bedroom and opened the front door to run. He did not return until hours later. I knew my sister, Wendy, was at the other end of the long ranch house that we lived in. She was now living in what was Grammy's apartment at the end of the house. I yelled, "Wendy! Wendy, come quickly! Dad is killing Mom!" Wendy ran over and kicked Dad right in his private area; he bent over, and Mom got free.

I cried and cried as all these emotions started surfacing from when I was little. Other things I had stuffed down while growing up also started to be released. I did not know how to deal with this. I had two little girls, eight and six, but I was feeling like I was a little girl myself and just did not know how to cope.

I had a very hard time falling asleep that night, but I finally did. At one point, I was standing in my bathroom, right off from my bedroom, and I could see Phil was sleeping. As I stood in front of the sink and looked down, all I could see was blood everywhere. My wrists were cut, and blood was pouring out. Then I woke up. It was just a dream! It was just a dream! I cried again, and Phil woke up, put his arm around me and did not say a word as I cried. After a long time, I finally drifted off to sleep. I had many dreams during this stage of life and did not know if they were real or not. I also dreamed of long-ago things I had forgotten about, and then I would wake up crying again!

At one point, I was dreaming that I was driving down the

road in my brown Dodge Aries, and there was a red pick-up truck coming directly at me. It kept coming at me, and I did not know what to do. I could not get out of the way, and the more I tried to get out of the way of the oncoming car, the driver kept coming right at me. Finally, he hit me head on! I woke up crying again.

"The doctors said I would never remember the drunk driver in the pickup truck who hit me," I exclaimed as I remembered this incident with tears streaming down my face. I did not get out of bed at all the next morning and well into the afternoon. I could hear Phil making phone calls out in the kitchen, and the frustration in his voice was very evident. He would let out a sigh of pure frustration as if to say, "Like what am I suppose to do?"

I heard Jay's voice, and I heard Phil say to him, "I am supposed to get her into a hospital, but I cannot find an opening."

"Where is she?" asked Jay.

"She's still in our room," Phil answered. Then Phil brought Jay into our room while Phil sat on one side of me and Jay on the other. "What's going on?" Jay asked me.

I went on telling him about the things I had been remembering. I was very comfortable with Jay and his wife, so it was not a problem for me to share this with him. "We will get through this together," said Jay, and I believed him. I knew that they would not leave Phil and me stranded with this. They took care of our girls and helped in whatever way they could for a very long time.

Later that day, Phil did manage to get in contact with a hospital that had an opening in the Psychiatric Department. Phil and Leona took me to the hospital, and I was asked all kinds of questions. As they were taking me to my room, I saw people whom I knew had some serious issues. I thought to myself, *They are crazy, and I am not. Why do I have to be here?* To be honest, the whole place was scary!

My room turned out to be dark; the whole unit was painted a dark color, but you would think it would have been warm and bright for people dealing with depression. There were two beds in my room. I had a roommate, an eighteen-year-old girl. There was also a desk in the room with a phone on it. The phone cord was about twelve inches long, but they should not have had a long cord in case someone wanted to use it as a noose for hanging. Right outside my bedroom window, I could see the helicopter pad where they would fly critical patients to the hospital.

The room phone rang and Phil answered it. It was my parents. "Your mom and Dad want to talk to you," said Phil.

"I don't know if I want to talk to them" was my response. In my mind, I was feeling like that little girl who was so afraid as a child; I was not feeling like a mother or a wife at all. I had just spent the past couple days having flashbacks of pain, hurt, and fear, and a lot of it was caused by Dad, so why would I want to talk to him? Phil and Leona encouraged me to talk to my parents, so I took the phone and said, "Hello!"

Dad responded, "Edna, I am sorry you are so sick. If you are sick from anything I have ever done, I am so sorry!"

The only thing I could say to Dad at that time was "Okay!" What did he want from me? Did he think I could just forgive him? The feelings were just too fresh and raw in my mind.

I got off the phone and then the nurse came in to check my suitcase. She took my 8 x 10 picture I had brought of Kelsey and Kendra and started taking it apart. Why are you doing that?" I asked.

"I need to take the glass out so you don't hurt yourself," she explained. It never would have occurred to me to use the glass from my daughters' picture frames to hurt myself, but this was the normal hospital procedure to ensure there was nothing in my personal belongings I could use as a weapon to hurt myself.

The nurse then told Phil and Leona they had to leave. "NO, NO, I don't want you to go!" I stated.

"I have to go, but I will be back tomorrow to see you," Phil replied.

"These people in here are crazy; I am not crazy. Why do I have to be here?" I asked. A look of torn emotions filled Phil's face as he walked out the door with Leona. Once they left, I threw myself on my bed and cried and screamed bitterly, "NO, NO, NO!" As I was crying and shaking with pain throbbing in my head, my roommate, the young eighteen-year-old girl, came over to me and said, "It will be okay! Here is something to help!" She handed me a stuffed Teddy bear. I grabbed the bear out of her hands and threw it across the room and screamed at her, "I don't need your bear; I need Jesus!" I must have known in my spirit that He was the only way out of this, but I had not even come to Him about all the feelings I was dealing with.

The nurse walked in the room as I was still crying inconsolably on my bed. "When you are done, you are required to come out for a group session with the other patients," she said. Her voice was cold and stern, and I thought to myself, *I don't want to go out there!*

The meeting room was right outside my room, so as soon as I opened the door, all these people were sitting directly in front of me. I took my seat, and the counselor began talking. She said that we were all to take a paper and pen and write ten things we liked about ourselves. *I do not have ten things I like about myself,* I thought. I sat there for a while thinking about this. *I don't like anything about myself at all. What do I write?* I wondered. I remember someone once telling me that I had pretty eyes, so that was one thing I guess I liked about myself. I wrote that on my list. Then, the thoughts that I went to church every Sunday and asked Jesus into my heart when I was eleven, and that I was a good person all came to mind, so I also put my relationship with Jesus Christ on my list.

A few minutes went by, and as people were writing things down, the counselor said that she now wanted everyone to share what they had written. "We will go around the room, taking turns", she explained.

It came to my turn. "I like my eyes and that I have a relationship with Jesus Christ," I said. "I only have two things on my list, and I cannot think of anything else to say," I explained. So they just moved on to the next person.

After the session was over, a man came up to me and said, "Thank you so much for sharing what you did. When I got here, I decided I was not going to talk to anyone at all, but since you said what you did about a relationship with Jesus Christ, it got me thinking that I need to work on that for myself. Thank you for sharing." The man walked away, and all I could wonder was why in the world I would have said that, because that was not the typical thing that I would say.

We had several group sessions a day, along with private sessions once a day with our psychiatric doctor. That night the nurse came to me and said, "Edna, come with me to the nurses' station. I want you to take some medication." As she handed me a pill cup and small glass of water, she instructed me to "Now go to bed, because this medication can make you sleepy."

"Okay," I responded. I swallowed the pill and then walked down the hall and around the corner to a small kitchen where there was juice in a refrigerator. I took a small glass of juice and drank it. Then I started down the hall toward my room. I remember getting to the lounge and seeing the door to my room, and that was the last of my memories about that part of the night..

All of a sudden, I heard the helicopter coming down. It was so loud, and the lights were glaring in my room. I sat up, shaking. The pain and the memories of being strapped down to a gurney and put into the helicopter from the car accident came rushing back like a flood. As I sat there shaking as the lights were flashing, I heard a voice like thunder say so clearly, and without a doubt, I knew it was God, "NO, you do not have a relationship with me!"

As I sat there at 2:30 in the morning, it was as if the Lord was doing a download on me and helping me realize the reason I was sick was because I had not come to Him and relied on Him. Therefore, I had no relationship with Him. Going to church on Sunday would not give me the relationship I needed to have with God. After this experience, I was wide awake. I went into the lounge and noticed a Gideon Bible, so I opened it up and thought, *What do I read*? I figured, *Well, Job went through a rough time. I will read about him.*

The next morning, I was asked to go the office of the psychiatric doctor. "I understand you did not sleep last night," he said.

"No!" I replied and then went on to tell him what had happened that night the Lord spoke to me. I assured him he could let me go home now, because I knew the reason I was sick and was aware of what I needed to get better.

With a very serious tone in his voice, he explained to

me, "You need to stay in the hospital longer and let the medication start working for you. I realize you needed to have this religious experience, but tonight I want to give you your medication and try to let it work so you can sleep.

"Okay," I responded. If I knew then what I know now, I would have never told him about the audible voice of the Lord that I heard. He thought I was really cracking up. I was given more and more medications. The pain in my head was awful, and because of the scar from my forehead back into my hairline, there was a tingly swelling with the headaches. I had to trust the doctors, because I had no other choice and did not know what else to do.

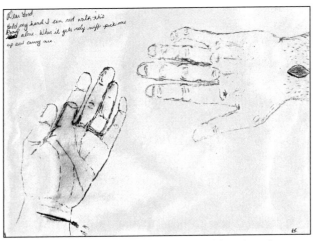

Vision Edna had while being prayed for when she kept seeing her wrists bloody.

If I am obedient and take the drugs, maybe I can go home quicker. I just want to get out of here, I thought to myself. At group sessions, they would tell us that depression was a disease and that suicide held one of the highest death rates in America. They taught us that we needed to accept what we could not change and simply take our medication. I was told that I had post traumatic stress disorder from remembering pain and trauma from the past. They explained to me that it is like what the Vietnam War veterans went through when they returned home; they would have flashbacks and did not know what to do at times. I was told that when the stress becomes too much, the memories can surface, causing a chemical imbalance in the brain. Medication, they said, was the best thing to correct my chemical imbalances.

God was also working on me, but I had no idea how much until later. I knew He would never leave me or forsake me, but at the time of my ordeal, I felt very alone and abandoned. Several times a day when I was in the hospital, these song lyrics kept coming to my mind:

> *"As the dear panteth for the water, so my heart longeth after thee.*
> *You alone are my heart's desire, and I long to worship thee.*
> *You alone are my strength and shield. To You alone may my spirit yield.*
> *You alone are my heart's desire, and I long to worship Thee."*
> Martin J. Nystrom (1981)

I never really thought too much about it at the time. I just knew that I liked the song and we sang it at church, but I had no idea at the time that the Lord was trying to tell me something.

> *"Why are you cast down , O my soul, and why are you disquieted within me? Hope in God; for I shall yet praise Him for the help of His countenance. O my God, my soul is cast down within me: Therefore I will remember You" (Ps. 42:5-6).*

Your soul is your mind, your will, and your emotions. Is your soul grieving? Are you sick or ashamed? There can be many things that can go wrong with our souls. Sometimes, it can be from pain, hurt, fear, emotions, trauma, unforgiveness, or even trying to please people rather than pleasing God. Most importantly, we need to realize that our loving Heavenly Father does not want us dealing with this. He longs for a deep, intimate relationship with Him. When our souls are sick, it blocks us from being so intimate with Him as He desires. I encourage you to pray:

Father, I need Your help! I know my soul is longing for more of You. Please, in Jesus' name, reveal to me what it is that is making my soul sick, and give me the courage and strength I need to give it to You. In Jesus' name, please take that problem and put it on the foot of the cross, cover it with the blood of Jesus Christ, and heal me whole, so that I can move forward in all that You have for me to walk in. With You walking by my side, I thank You and praise You in the precious name of Jesus. Amen!

My Soul Longed for You

CHAPTER 8

Hospitalized

I waited patiently for the Lord; and He inclined to me and heard my cry. He also brought me up out of a horrible pit, out of the miry clay, and set my feet upon a rock, and established my steps (Ps. 39:1-2).

As the days in the hospital passed, I tried to be different. I would pray at the meals and have everyone at my table bow their heads as I blessed the food; I thought the Lord wanted this of me. I am not sure what I was really thinking, but I knew that growing up as a Mennonite was about being a doer. We always did things: we helped, we served, we blessed, and as far as I knew, doing for others was the only way to have a relationship with Jesus Christ. So I was going to let the other patients at the hospital know that we should read the Bible and pray. I even gave my Bible to the young girl in my room, thinking she needed it more than I did.

I was in the hospital for a week, but it felt like an eternity. I missed Kelsey and Kendra so much. Questions floated through my mind that I had no answers for: *What must they think of their mother? Will they understand? Will I be able to do this when I get home?*

On the last day of my hospital stay, there was a new patient who came in that morning. I sat down next to her and asked her name. As she was about to tell me, she said, "I slit my wrists last night." I looked down and noticed that her wrists were bandaged up. Fear gripped me so strongly, and I could not shake it. I knew that Leona was scheduled to pick me up at the hospital that afternoon and that there was no way I was going to tell any doctor or counselor there that since I had talked with this woman, I kept seeing my wrists bloody. They would never let me get out of there. I was going home that day no matter what!

Leona arrived at the hospital to pick me up, and the doctor released me, making sure I had all my prescriptions. He told us to get them filled and stay faithful with taking all five medications. Before going home, Leona and I went to Walmart to get the prescriptions filled. As she and I were sitting in McDonald's waiting for the prescriptions, I kept seeing my wrists bloody. Leona was talking about all the events going on at church, including the Power team being at the local high school and that everyone enjoyed them. I interrupted her, and with fear in my voice, said, "Leona, stop talking! I need you to pray for me. I need you to pray now! I keep seeing my wrists bloody, and it will not stop since I talked to that woman this morning who had slit her wrists."

Concern filled Leona's brown eyes. "Did you tell the doctor this?" she asked.

"No, I was not going to tell the doctor, because if I had, he would have never let me leave today, and I want to go home . . . so pray for me!" Leona took my hands and started to pray that day in McDonald's. I have no idea what she prayed, but all I know is that when my eyes were shut, I could see my bloody wrists so clearly. As she continued to pray, the image I saw was no longer my wrists bloody but Jesus high-priced stained wrists, and His hands were reaching for mine. Peace came over me, and I knew that I needed a relationship with Jesus more than ever to heal my heart.

When I got home, I slept a lot. The girls were at school, and then someone from the church would take them. I was not myself. "This medication makes me feel worse than I was in the first place; it makes me feel more depressed," I explained to Phil.

He reminded me that the depression medication, Prozac, would take at least five weeks to take full effect, as this is what the doctors at the hospital told us. I hated trying to fall asleep, because everything would be quiet, and then if there was just a slight noise anywhere in the house, it would go through me like a knife. I felt a sharpness as if my nerves were just flying together, and my heart racing. *How can I rest like this?* I wondered.

I felt so many strange things; I just did not feel like myself. I was so tired all the time. Even taking a shower would be so tiring. The doctor told me that after going through depression like I did, was like I had gone through major surgery and my body would take time to regain its full strength. The tension was building up more and more all the time.

One night the phone rang and Phil answered it. It was the young girl who had been my roommate at the hospital. She simply wanted to talk with me. I listened as she went on telling me about her boyfriend and how it did not work with him and what she was doing now that she was also out of the hospital. As she talked, I began getting a very strong sensation all over my body as if something had come down on top of me. Prickly pain went from the back of my head all the way down my back, and I thought I was not going to get to the bathroom in time. I abruptly told the young girl I had to go and hung up the phone. Then, I dashed to the bathroom and made it just in time. My chest was so tight from the pain, fear, and shortness of breath. I started to scream. "Phil! Phil, I am dying! Help me! Help me! I do not know what to do! I am dying!"

Phil quickly ran to the phone and called 911. He told them what was going on as best as he could and where we lived. Then he came to our bedroom where I was on the floor. I would get on the bed and then down on the floor again. "What is wrong with me? I am going to die!" I screamed. The fear and pain was so intense from the prickly feelings up and down my spine and head. My heart was racing, and I kept running to the bathroom. I started to dehydrate quickly, and when I talked, white foamy saliva came out.

As the EMT came walking in, I recognized him and knew he was also a pastor at a nearby church who lived just on the other side of the hill from us, so he got to us before the ambulance did. "Pray for me! Pray for me! I am dying," I said to him. As he took my hand and prayed, others from the EMT came in and put me on the stretcher to take me out to the ambulance. "Phil, where are the girls?" I asked.

"They're in bed," he said. "Jay and Nellene are coming over to stay with them."

At the hospital, after evaluating my heart, I was told that I was not having a heart attack but a panic attack. The doctor asked Phil which medications I was on, and he asked me if I had been taking them all. However, because of his foreign accent, I could not understand him. When I asked him to repeat what he said, he asked again and again while getting more stern with me for not answering his question. But I just could not understand him, and I was so afraid by this point that it was almost impossible to be calm.

Just then, I heard Leona's voice out in the waiting room, and I screamed as loudly as I could, "Leona, I need you now!" Finally, after Phil realized what the doctor had been saying, he explained it to me. Then I let the doctor know I had not been taking all the medication, because it made me feel weird.

"You must take all of it; that is why you had this attack," he said.

As the days went on, I started to feel less and less like myself. I was angry all the time, and my thoughts were not good. I started wondering more and more if I should kill myself. I felt worse than ever before. Kelsey and Kendra were with Jay and Nellene or other people in the church more than they were at home. I was afraid to be alone with them because I was so angry inside. I would tell Phil, "I feel like someone is trapped in my body making me feel and do things that are not me." I was scared of my temper; I always had a temper, and it would flare up when fear gripped me. Now, it was even worse, because my out-of-control feeling had increased significant. *What is wrong with me?* I couldn't stop wondering.

One afternoon when feeling that I had reached just about all I could take of this torment in my soul, I went outside to the top of the hill in our backyard and cried. I did not care if the neighbors heard me, because that was the last thing on my mind. I just wanted relief. I stood there crying and shaking, and then I hollered as loudly as I could, "God, where are You? What do You want from me? I can't do this anymore!"

My thoughts were so fast-moving all the time that I would constantly ask Phil questions. His reply would always be, "I don't know; ask Jay." Phil did not know how to help me, and he did not know what to say to me. This was especially hard for him since he already had a very hard time communicating before all this, so this just made it worse at times. Phil would go with me to the counselor, but that would not help me at all. The counselor would ask me all kinds of questions, and then my time would be up and I would have to go home and try to deal with the pain of the questions asked about my past. Phil would call Jay before work in the mornings and let him know how I was doing. If I was not doing well, he would ask Jay to call or check on me some time during the day. Phil worked an hour away, so he could not just come home to check on me or even call, as there were no phones on the job sites where he was building.

One day the phone rang, and it was a friend from the area of Pennsylvania where we used to live. She had also been dealing with some depression. As she talked, I felt more helpless. I could not be of any help to her, because I couldn't even help myself. I hung up the phone and all alone, I cried and screamed and just wanted to end my life. I had no hope. Yes, I loved my girls, but I was not good enough for them, and I could not live this way any longer. The torment was getting worse by the day. I screamed and cried, rolling back and forth while curled up in a fetal potion thinking about how would I do this? How could I just end this pain. The next thing I knew, Jay walked in the room and held me and said, "It's okay. It's okay. Stop your crying! We are going to get through this! It's okay."

My crying finally slowed down, and I realized I was not alone. "Edna, I don't know what to tell you to do," said Jay. "I do not know how to help you, and I want to more than anything, but I cannot fix this. The only thing I know to do is to pray." As Jay prayed for me, I remembered the reason I was sick was because I needed to have a relationship with Christ.

"Jay, I know that I need to put all this at the foot of the cross, but I don't know how," I said. I knew in my heart that when these panic attacks would arise, Satan himself was after me. It was as if Satan was brutally tormenting me, and the fear was like nothing I had ever experienced. I asked the pastor if I could be anointed with oil. I knew God had dramatically healed me when I was in the car accident, so I believed He would do so again. I told Leona I was ready for whatever was going to happen, and I was not referring to suicide when I said I would be healed. Either living or dying, I knew I would be healed.

After that, things started to change a little bit, but I also knew it was the medication causing a lot of the problems. I believe the Lord was with me all the way through, and Satan wanted my soul more than anything.

For God has not given us a spirit of fear, but of power, and of love, and of a sound mind (2 Tim. 1:7).

There is no fear in love, but perfect love casts out fear, because fear involves torment. But he who fears has not been made perfect in love (1 John 4:18).

Do you have fear in your life? Do you desire to know the love of the Father like I did? When fear grips you so hard that you don't even know how to function, it affects your soul, your spirit, and your body. It can make you physically sick, and it drives a wedge between you and your Heavenly Father, a wedge that He does not want us to have, a wedge that we should not want, either.

I encourage you to take this verse from 2 Timothy and speak it over yourself daily, so it can get into your spirit and soul:

For God has not given us a spirit of fear, but of power, and of love, and of a sound mind (2 Tim. 1:7).

My Soul Longed for You

CHAPTER 9

Depending on the Lord

Casting down all your cares upon Him, for He cares for you. Be sober, be vigilant because your adversary the devil walks about like a roaring lion, seeking whom he may devour (1 Pt. 5:7-8).

On Sunday morning, as I woke up to yet another panic attack, Phil called Jay and Nellene. They came over before they went to church to help with the girls and to pray until I got through the panic attack. I never knew how long an attack would last. As I was sitting there with fear gripping me. Phil was holding one hand and Jay the other.

Jay said, "Edna, look at the daffodil Nellene and I brought for you. It is spring, and God is giving you new life just as He is giving this daffodil new life." I held on to those words and kept reminding myself that God was giving me new life. "Edna, every morning when you wake up, I want you to say, 'This is the day the Lord has made, and I will rejoice and be glad in it,' (Ps. 118:24)," Jay said with such confidence. He knew that if I chose to think and speak positive, it would help me to make positive choices.

I finally got my medication changed from Prozac to a different depression drug. I now had a Christian doctor and regular checkups and was also going to a different Christian counselor. Phil and I would visit the counselor together, and even though it was tough, it was a good thing for us to do.

We were starting to communicate, which was something that was lacking in our marriage. Also, Phil was making decisions more often than he had been, which was another wonderful improvement for our relationship.

Kelsey was only eight at the time, and there was still something about her that I had noticed and admired since she was a small child; she never needed to go to a person to deal with her pain or her doubt. She knew in her spirit to go to the Lord. One day while Kelsey was outside playing, she walked into the woods and found a rock to sit on. As she sat, she asked Jesus to come into her heart.

Kelsey Cassel standing in back, Kendra Cassel sitting next to Edna Cassel, and Phil Cassel behind.

Kelsey was baptized that summer, and she always had a confidence about her that was truly from God. She never had a desire to be like others, and even when peer pressure surrounded her, she stood out and was okay with being different from her friends. Growing up, she would continuously seek the Lord about things before telling anyone else. I admired this about her, and when I was dealing with all my torment, I wondered how she had such strong faith when I did not even know how to deal with life and put my pain at the foot of the cross. "And a little child will lead them" (Isa. 11:6).

I told my Christian doctor that I wanted to depend on the Lord, not the drugs. He helped me to wean off all the extra medications. Eventually, I was just taking the depression medication. I was feeling a lot better now that I had been taken off of Prozac. The new medication helped me feel like everything was brighter and sharper. A cloud had lifted, and I was seeing things more clearly than I had in a long time.

I also stopped working at the school and got a job assisting an elderly woman while the girls were in school. I did this job for three years. During that time, I grew into an understanding that there was a deeper walk with the Lord than I had known in the past. When I went to the elderly lady's house to work, I would help her get up in the morning, fix her breakfast, and then I would read the Scriptures to her. It was a God set-up, but I did not realize at the time how much God was watching out and working on my soul to lead me into a deeper walk with Him.

As I read devotions to the lady I helped care for, she would pour her wisdom and love for the Lord into me. "Edna, I fell in love with Jesus," she would often say. I had never heard any others say that they had fallen in love with Jesus. It made me wonder how that was possible. At times, it seemed as if my prayers where hitting the ceiling. Questions about how to have a relationship with Jesus would go through my mind, but how to fall in love with Him was a whole new concept for me.

I realized I was trying to have a relationship with Christ in the physical instead of simply falling in love with Him. I believe this is how religion works; it pushes us to think of what we can do to create that relationship with Christ while not helping us to understand that He has already given us this special relationship with Him as a free gift. Then, we are open to receive life more abundantly if we simply surrender, obey, and walk in the Spirit.

The next three years were spent renewing my mind. Phil often told me that I think too much. So, with all that thinking, I had to learn to bring it under captivity to the Lord Jesus Christ. Philippians 4:8, says, "Finally, my brethren, whatever things are true, whatever things are noble, whatever things are just, whatever things are pure, whatever things are lovely, whatever things are of good report, if there is any virtue and if there is anything praiseworthy, meditate on these things."

I would measure my thoughts by this standard, and if they were not true, noble, just, pure, lovely, and of good report, I would demand, "Satan, get behind me!" My thoughts were slower, and it was a long process, but I was starting to make decisions for myself again, and it was not as big of a chore like it was when I first came out of the hospital.

Although my thinking was improving, I wasn't always making the right choices, because I was following my feelings more than the truth. I needed to learn truth as the Bible explains in Philippians 4:8 (quoted above). No one can know what the truth is without knowing the Word, because the Word is truth, and Christ is the Word explained in John 1:1-5. Reading the Bible was not an easy task for me; I did not like to read and neither did Phil. Reading on my own strength was not going to happen.

Casting all your care upon Him, for He cares for you. Be sober, be vigilant, because your adversary the devil walks about like a roaring lion, seeking whom he may devour. Resist him, steadfast in the faith, knowing that the same sufferings are experiencing by your brotherhood in the world. But may the God of all grace, who called us to His eternal glory by Christ Jesus, after you have suffered a while, perfect, establish, strengthen, and settle you. To Him be the glory and the dominion forever and ever. Amen (1 Pt. 5:7-11).

For the weapons of our warfare are not carnal but mighty in God for pulling down strongholds, casting down arguments and every high thing that exalts itself against the knowledge of God, bringing every thought into captivity to the obedience of Christ, and being ready to punish all disobedience when your obedience is fulfilled (2 Cor. 10: 4-5).

I had to cast down a lot of high things that were in my mind. Stinking thinking, things I thought were true were just lies from the Enemy. It is not easy to bring every thought into captivity to the obedience of Christ; it's a lifelong process. Our desire should be that we want to be walking in obedience with our Lord and Savior. The more we put our thoughts into captivity and ask the Lord to reveal wrong thoughts through His Word, the freer we will become.

I encourage you to take a step toward this goal, and you will start thinking more slowly, an important habit to form. I am not saying the process of renewing your mind will be easy. In fact, it may get harder at times, because the adversary will challenge you, but if you resist the devil through prayer and standing firm on the truth of God's Word, you will break through!

My Soul Longed for You

CHAPTER 10

One with God

Bless the Lord, O my soul, and all that is within me, bless His holy name. Bless the Lord, O my soul, and forget not all His benefits, who forgives all your inequities, who heals all your diseases, who redeems your life from destruction, who crowns you with loving kindness and tender mercies, who satisfies your mouth with good things so that your youth is renewed like the eagle's (Ps. 103:1-5).

A few years after the depression, I was doing fine but still wondering how to have a relationship with Jesus Christ. One night at the weekly small-group Bible study at the Mennonite church, I was asked if I would lead the next lesson for the following week. I accepted, and at this time we were studying different characters in the Bible. The story of Deborah in Judges 4 and 5 would be the lesson I was to lead. I did not read much at the time, but I was so intrigued with Deborah that I wanted to be like her, because she could hear from God. In the book we were following, it said that Deborah was one with God.

As we were sitting around the kitchen table the next week for Bible study, I started to read the Scriptures and ask the questions listed in the study book. Excitement started rising up inside of me. "Deborah was one with God. She could hear God. She knew what He wanted her to do," I joyfully exclaimed to those in my study group. "If Deborah can be one with God, then we can be one with God."

My excitement was at such a high level that I just wanted to shout. "If God is the same now as He was then, then it is possible for us to be one with God," I blurted out. "This means that we can hear God, too!" The excitement of hearing from God and knowing what He wanted us to do was huge for me, because it seemed I had previously heard from God in a not-so-positive way. Now all I wanted was to be one with Him in a positive way.

That week, when Phil and I went to the counselor for my weekly appointment, I asked, "How do I become one with God like Deborah?"

"You still have unforgiveness, Edna! The only way you can become one with God is for you to forgive those who have hurt you," the counselor explained. I was puzzled, because I thought I had forgiven the drunk who hit my car, along with my dad and the men who hit on me in the past when I was a young girl and when I was married. Who else was there to forgive? The counselor went on to say that he was going to pray that God would reveal to me who else I had not forgiven and that God would give me the strength to forgive them.

The following week, I got mini flashbacks of things and people. During those moments, I needed to ask myself if I had forgiven the person who came to mind. Since I was so much stronger by now, I realized that it was far more important to be one with God than it was to hold on to unforgiveness. I knew that harboring unforgiveness was eating me up inside and destroying my soul, and that did not measure up with Philippians 4:8.

The Lord reminded me of the time when I was sixteen, before my car accident. I was driving home from work one evening during a bad storm. Tree limbs were falling all around me, the wind was blowing, and the rain was coming down so hard that I could hardly see. I just wanted to get home and not be driving in that bad weather. I finally got to our house and ran through the rain to the front door, but the door was locked. I stood there banging on the door and calling out, "Mom! Mom! Let me in!" I could hear Mom and Dad inside and could not understand why they would not let me in.

"Don't you open that door," I heard Dad say to Mom. I banged on the door and called out some more, but since no one opened it, I ran back to my car. There I sat, soaking wet, until the storm was over. While waiting out the storm, I went somewhere else in my mind like I would do when I was scared. I do not know how long the storm lasted, but it seemed like quite some time before it stopped. When it was over, I returned to the house, knocked again, and Mom opened it this time. "Why would you not open the door for me?" I asked Dad who was sitting in his rocking chair.

"I did not want the door to blow in from the storm," Dad answered.

"But I was outside getting all wet and needed to come in," I replied.

"I didn't want the door to blow in!" Dad repeated. I stood there confused and hurt while thinking, *How could the door being blown in be more important than me?*

As this memory was flooding my mind, I started to wonder why Mom didn't protect me and why she wouldn't just open the door. *I am her daughter. Shouldn't she protect me?* I questioned. Then it hit me like a ton of bricks that I was still holding resentment toward my mom, the one who always treated me so well, and the one whom I knew loved me. I went to my room and threw myself across my bed and asked the Lord to forgive me for holding resentment and hurt toward my mom.

I confronted my mother shortly after that and asked her why she did not let me in the house during that storm many years ago when I was sixteen. "I was too scared to open the door," she explained. I then understood, because fear had also stopped me from doing many things in the past. Her response made it easier for me to let go completely of any bitterness I was holding toward her. I found forgiveness, and it was a time of cleansing for my soul.

> "For if you forgive men their trespasses, your heavenly Father will also forgive you. But if you do not forgive men their trespasses, neither will your Father forgive your trespasses" (Matt. 6:14-15).

> "You shall love the Lord your God with all your heart, with all your soul, with all your strength, and with all your mind, and your neighbor as yourself" (Luke 10:27).

Many people hold on to unforgiveness for many reasons, and it was clear that God was working on my soul to clean me up so that I could be one with Him. That was my strong desire. Sometimes we hold on to unforgiveness without even realizing it, like an offense toward someone. The Lord does not want us to be offended by others. The stronger I got to know who I was in Christ, the more clearly I realized that I needed to keep myself clean from unforgiveness. If we love the Lord with all our heart, soul, mind, and strength, and if we love our neighbor as ourselves like God asks us to, then we should be confident that we will be able to forgive and love the way God designed us to. Both forgiveness and love are choices God expects from His children.

Is there something you are holding on to that is preventing you from forgiving and loving someone? Maybe you think that if you don't chose to forgive and love, you are punishing the other person, but that mindset is only punishing you. The Lord is gracious to us, and when we chose to forgive, no matter how big or how small the offense is, in His love and mercy, He will help us to chose to forgive. Then, there will be no block between our Heavenly Father and us. So keep seeking Him as your strength, and stand on the Word as He shows you the way.

CHAPTER 11

The Ring

For this reason I bow my knee to the Father of our Lord Jesus Christ, from whom the whole family in heaven and earth is named, that He would grant you, according to the riches of His glory, to be strengthened with might through His Spirit in the inner man. That Christ may dwell in your hearts through faith, that you, being rooted and grounded in love, may be able to comprehend with all the saints what is the width and length and depth and height, to know the love of Christ which passes knowledge, that you may be filled with all the fullness of God (Eph. 3:14-19).

As Phil and I were sitting in the counselor's office, the counselor reminded me again about stepping back and taking a look at my reactions. *What is it that is making me react the way I do? What is the real reason I am feeling the way I do? What is the root problem?* These were different questions I would have to ask as I went through my day, and then with whatever the answer to the root problem was, I would measure it according to Philippians 4:8.

We talked about my dad and the way he was when I was young. Because of the type of relationship I had with him and Phil's lack of encouraging words to me, I was seeing my self-worth through other people's eyes, based on what they said I was or how they treated me.

"Edna, you cannot find your identity in anyone else!" the counselor explained. "You are not Edna in your dad. You are not Edna in Phil. You are Edna in Christ!" The counselor went on to explain that my dad was my biological dad and not my real dad. "Only your Heavenly Father is your real dad," he taught me. "Think of the most amazing father figure . . . what you think a great dad would be. Well, that is what your Heavenly Father is to you, but even so much more. Edna, find your identity in Christ, not in man!" he reiterated. WOW! That hit me like a ton of bricks, because I knew I always tried to please everyone. I thought my self-worth came from pleasing people, so they would think good of me.

That afternoon, after Phil and I left the counselor, Phil was driving and pulled into the parking lot of a strip mall. He said we were going to buy a ring. We went into the store and I picked out a sterling silver ring. Back in the car, Phil said with love in his voice, "Edna, I want you to wear this ring all the time. And every time you look at it, I want you to remember that you are 'Edna in Christ!'"

Earlier that day, the counselor had mentioned that people in the Old Testament wore items on their garments to show their identity. He mentioned that some people still do that by wearing a ring or another visible item that can be seen often and serves as a reminder. I was so thankful that Phil thought this would be a good reminder for me, and since I am a visual person, it worked great.

Do you try to define yourself through others by trying to please them? I thought that if I could just please people, I would be better off. At the same time, I had a warped understanding of what was expected of relationships. I thought I should please others to be loved, but I soon found out that a mindset like that can make you believe that others should try to please you, too.

There was no way that Phil could be all I would ever need. Although he's a great husband who loves and cares for me, he is a person, and all of our needs cannot be met through another person. Our Heavenly Father is the only one who can meet our needs and the only one who should meet all our needs. As a people-pleaser, I depended on people way too much instead of on the Lord, so God had to show me that if I was going to be one with Him (like Deborah was), I needed to depend on Him as the source of who I am, and I am Edna in Christ!

There have been a few times over the years that I caught myself slipping back into my old mindset, but God and His love reminded me of His truth and in whom to be putting all my trust. I encourage you to pray and ask our Heavenly Father to help you to rely on Him and His love to mold you into the person He has called you to be.

Also, reading Ephesians 3:14-19 can help. You can personalize those verses and then read them daily to allow this concept to get into your spirit and soul. As He works in your inner man to know His love, you will be molded into the person Christ wants you to be, and you will know the love of Christ which passes knowledge and renews your mind.

"Be renewed in the spirit of your mind" (Eph. 4:23).

My Soul Longed for You

The Gift

"Likewise the Spirit also helps in our weakness, for we do not know what we should pray for as we ought, but the Spirit Himself makes intercession for us with groaning which cannot be uttered" (Rom. 8:26).

The next few years came with the slow process of finding my identity, learning to think like Philippians 4:8, and a lot of physical pain. I had to have several surgeries dealing with the endometrioses, and finally, when I turned thirty-two, I had a hysterectomy. The thought would often enter my mind that it was a punishment for not asking God how many children He wanted us to have.

Finally, by the summer of 2005, I was doing great. I was no longer going to the counselor, and I was working and keeping things together pretty well. But there was this deep longing I had that let me know what I wanted more than anything, and that was to be one with God like Deborah, to have a relationship with Jesus Christ. I just felt in my spirit that there had to be more.

I asked one of the sweet, dear ladies in our church who understood the Bible well if she would keep me accountable and if we could go through the Word and study together. She was a blessing, and we started to meet every week. Before we knew it, other women were joining us. It was a good time of reading the Word and discussing what it had to say to us. I did not understand a lot of what I was reading, but I knew I had to read it if I was going to know Jesus better.

During this time, a friend invited me to a women's retreat at Back Rock Retreat. This was the same place that my mother had visited before I was born and accepted Jesus as her savior. This was not a Mennonite gathering, although it was a Mennonite woman who asked me to go; she was always looking for more of Jesus. She told me that this retreat was held annually at Black Rock and that she was always glad she went. I went and was blessed. I enjoyed it so much that I scheduled to go again the following year. That time, I took Nellene with me and met up with my mom and a friend.

The worship there was so good. Some ladies would raise their hands while singing and others would not. I believe there were several denominations present at this retreat, but the ones that spoke and did the singing impressed me the most. They would share, give testimonies, and then we would break up in small groups and pray. It was a refreshing weekend. On the last day of the retreat during our last speaking session, one of the retreat leaders said there were gifts on a table near her that had been prayed over for the past several months. There was a specific gift for each woman in attendance. We were told that the gift we were drawn to most was the one we should pick. There were about 100 women there, so the table was full of gifts of all colors. Some were in gift bags and some in baskets. A specific one caught my eye, and as I walked forward in the line of women to get it, the woman in front of me grabbed it. Disgusted, I figured I would just grab the basket next to it.

I returned to my seat to open my gift. As other women were opening their gifts, you would hear them laughing because of the gift they had received or crying because it meant so much to them. Mine was a very small basket, and inside was a folded piece of paper. I unfolded it and read the word *intercession* on it. *What?* I thought to myself. *What in the world is intercession?* I had never even heard of the word and was so disappointed that I didn't at least get something that I knew was for me. The word made no sense to me, and if all these gifts were prayed over so carefully to be matched specifically with each woman there, why did mine have so little to do with me?

Women were lining up to give testimonies about the great gifts they had received and how God had spoken to them through these gifts. I just sat there listening. While I was happy for the other women, I couldn't help thinking that I got gypped. The following week when I went to work at the home of the elderly lady I cared for, I visited her study, because I knew she had lots of books. As I perused the titles, one jumped out at me called *Intercession*. There was that word again, so I pulled the book off the shelf and began reading it while my client took her nap. I quickly got bored, though, since I did not understand what I was reading. I finally just stopped reading and decided that I was not going to figure out what the word meant or what it had to do with me.

"Therefore He is also able to save to the uttermost those who come to God through Him, since He always lives to make intercession for them" (Heb. 7:25).

Jesus Christ is making intercession for us; He is standing in the gap for us. He interceded for us on the cross where He took the punishment of our sins (see Is. 53:12). He also is praying to the Father for us, and isn't that just the most awesome thought? He is our go-between.

"Likewise the Spirit also helps in our weakness for we do not know what we should pray for as we ought, but the Spirit Himself makes intercession for us with groaning

which cannot be uttered. Now He who searches the heart knows what the mind of the Spirit is because He makes intercession for the saints according to the will of God. And we know that all things work together for good to those who love God, to those who are the called to His purpose" (Rom. 8: 26-28).

What a faithful promise! Many people quote part of this verse: "All things work together for good to those who love the Lord," but, there is so much more to it! There were so many times I would groan and cry not knowing what to pray or how to pray, but the Holy Spirit knew just what to pray for me.

Later, I found out that the Holy Spirit was more than just a new Spirit when I accepted Christ so I would not go to hell. I learned that He is my helper who knows what I do not know. He knows the will of God, and that is how all things work together for good to those who love Him.

CHAPTER 13

Witnessing

"For I am not ashamed of the gospel of Christ, for it is the power of God to salvation for everyone who believes, for the Jews first and also for the Greeks" (Rom. 1:16).

A man from the community came to the church one Sunday morning and asked our pastor if he could have a few minutes to share before the sermon. As we were all sitting in church, this man got up and began talking about leading people to Christ at the Troy Fair. He was so excited and exuberant as he talked that I seriously did not know if I had ever seen a man so excited about being saved.

He explained that he was going to all the local churches to ask the congregations to join in with leading people to Christ. There would be shifts all week long, so people were needed at the fair at all times. I did not even mind that this man was more emotional than what I was used to seeing in church, and I could not shake the fact that he would ask us to go out witnessing like that. There was a sign-up sheet at the back of the church for those who wanted to help. I did not sign my name, but by the time Wednesday came, as I was sitting with the ladies from Bible study, I could not shake that feeling that I should do this.

One of the ladies said that she and her husband had signed up. "I just can't stop thinking about it," I explained. "Maybe I should go."

"I have that man's phone number if you want to call him," a lady said to me. "I am sure it's not too late, because the fair starts on Friday."

I thanked the lady and took the phone number home with me. The next day, I made the call. When I explained to the man who answered how I couldn't stop thinking about this opportunity at the fair, I could hear the excitement in his voice. He went on to explain how he and some others would do the witnessing, and they would have a tent set up where the helpers would hand out tracts and pray with people. He recited the Ten Commandments and said that the people at the fair would be given the Commandments on a walking stick or bracelet made of colored beads. The color *black* would represent sin; *red*, the blood of Jesus; *white* would represent Jesus washing our sins as white as snow; *green*, living a life of Christ; and *gold* would be for the streets of gold that we would go to someday.

The explanation of how they were planning to lead people at the fair to Christ was very interesting, and I had never heard it explained that way before. When I got off the phone, with tears running down my face, I confessed sin in my life that I knew God would not want there. If I was going to move forward and lead others to Christ, how could I stand there explaining salvation with sin in my own life?

When Friday came, I told the girls we are going to go to the fair and that Daddy would pick them up after work. I explained to them what we would be doing at the fair. They were not sure what to think at first, but once we arrived at the fair, they saw firsthand what was going on, such as seeing several people in the tent praying with others. *I can do this! I am outgoing*, I thought to myself, so I went up to the first person who turned out to be a willing listener. But I stumbled over my words and felt like I was just speaking something that had been memorized. I sat down in the back of the tent, crying, "Jesus, I can't do this by myself. You need to give me the words to say, because I can't say and do this on my own. Please speak through me."

The man I had talked to on the phone saw that I was struggling and suggested I first observe him talking with someone. He thought that perhaps I'd feel more comfortable doing this process as a team. "Yes! I think that sounds like a good idea," I said.

He started chatting with an older gentlemen in dirty old jeans who wore a ponytail. He asked him if he wanted to sit and talk in the tent. As we sat, I heard the plan of salvation being explained, and I watched this scruffy old guy with his dirty clothes and long ponytail. He started to get the most sincere look on his face and began weeping in a way I had never seen a man cry before. As the old guy got down on his knees, he cried out, confessing his sins and saying, "Father, forgive me for I have sinned, and I need You as my Lord and Savior." I was kneeling beside him and so was the leader. Tears ran down my face, and for the first time, I saw there was way more to life than I ever thought, and that was reaching souls for the Kingdom.

I was so excited when I got home. "Phil, I want to do this for the rest of my life. There is nothing better than seeing people on their knees crying out for a Savior," I exclaimed. I was so excited that I could not even sleep that night. I got to thinking, *Yes, I am going to Bible study now, but I need to know what this Bible says if I am going to be telling people about Jesus.* At the fair, we were suggesting that people start reading John and then Romans, so that's just what I did that night and then went on to the other books of the Bible. I was up until 3 a.m.

I went again the next day and had Kelsey and Kendra hand out tracts to people. They would say, "If you want to know how to receive Jesus as your savior, you can talk to my mommy. She is in the tent." I told my daughters that they were my *fishers of men*, and that I was so proud of them wanting to help and be a part of this.

That week, I went to the fair every day and stayed until 11 p.m. Then, I would come home and read the Scriptures until two or three in the morning. Phil came to the fair one night, but I could tell that he was extremely uncomfortable doing this, so he would pick up the girls from the fair in the evening, and I would stay on leading people to Christ. I led twenty-two people to Christ that week, and then two weeks later we went to another fair in the next county, which was a totally different experience. The people there were not as open as those at the Troy Fair had been. Some of those on our team who had done this many times before said some of us must just stay to the side of the tent and pray.

Then Jesus said to those Jews who believed Him, "If you abide in My word, you are My disciples indeed; and you shall know the truth, and the truth shall make you free" (John 8: 31-32).

CHAPTER 14

Holy Spirit Baptism

"I indeed baptized you with water, but He will baptize you with the Holy Spirit" (Mark 1:8).

The Bible study was going very well, and we had gone through two books of the Bible. Both were very interesting even though I did not understand them like I wanted to. But at least I was growing and learning more. We started to study the Book of Acts when I began noticing that not all of us were seeing eye to eye on what we were reading. We read about John being baptized with water, but you shall be baptized with the Holy Spirit and that you would receive power when the Holy spirit comes upon you. We also read about the Day of Pentecost when the Holy Spirit came and there appeared like tongues of fire on them, and they were filled with the Holy Spirit and spoke in other tongues.

I went home that afternoon as if I had just discovered some newfound miracle. I was so excited for Phil to get home, so I could read it to him. *Surely, Phil would want to hear what I was reading in Acts and be excited,* I imagined. When he arrived home from work, we told the girls to go and play so we could sit and talk. Phil sat down on the sofa next to me, and I told him that we were studying Acts in Bible study and that I wanted to read something to him. I went on to read about the Holy Spirit coming and giving us power. I told Phil that I thought that there must be more than salvation, that

God must have more for us than just forgiving our sins, and that there must be a baptism where we would receive power.

I read some more and then asked, "So, what do you think?" Phil looked at me with total disgust in his eyes and said, "If you don't quit it, you are going to turn me off." I could not understand why he was not excited as I was, but I knew enough not to mention it to him again.

I started praying all the time that Phil would be hungry for more and that he would want a relationship with Jesus Christ like I did. I continued to pray that prayer for six months. During that time, I started a new job at Troy Hospital as a nurse's aide, taking care of people in the skilled unit. I prayed, "God, please give me a job where I can witness to people. I don't want a job to make money; I want a job where I can make difference."

After two weeks of being a nurse's aide, my boss came to me and asked if I would consider being the activities coordinator. She explained that I would interview each new patient and have activities for them to do. If they were there for therapy, I would give them an activity that would help them to be more mobile, which would help the therapists. She also told me that I would be in charge of the volunteers by being the volunteer coordinator. "Edna, you have the right personality for this job," she said.

I went home and told Phil about it and prayed about it. If I didn't take the job, I was afraid I would regret it, so the next day, I accepted the position.

There was chapel each Wednesday at the hospital. Local pastors from the churches in the area took turns with chaplain duty. On Wednesday, I would make rounds at the hospital asking the patients if they would like to attend chapel, and then I would take them in their wheelchairs to the chapel.

One day when I was wheeling the patients into the chapel, I noticed a chaplain I had not seen before. I waited with the patients as I always did in case they needed anything. While there, I heard a very meaningful message from the chaplain that day and noticed that when he finished, he laid his hands on the patients while praying such a sincere prayer with confidence that the prayer would be answered. He knelt down on his knees to look into the patients' eyes as he spoke to them and made them feel important.

"What is your name?" I asked.

"Josh Payne," he replied. "I am the pastor at Victory Church."

"What is it about you? You are different from the other pastors who come in and speak to the patients." He stood there with a great big smile as his blue eyes glowed. He never answered but only said he would be back the next day to visit the patients.

One day I got a call from Edna Zimmerman who was the other "Edna" in my Bible Study group. She asked if Phil and I would come over to her house to hear a pastor from a church in Troy speak about baptism in the Holy Spirit. That night, I told Phil that Edna was wondering if we would come over to her house to meet a pastor and hear what he had to say about the Holy Spirit. I was nervous about what Phil would say, remembering my not-so successful talk with him about the Holy Spirit six months earlier. He thought for a second and said, "I guess we can go."

That night, when we arrived at Edna and her husband's house, it was Josh, the pastor from Victory Church who was there. Josh greeted Phil and gave him a warm welcome. A full table of people gathered to hear what this pastor had to say about the Holy Spirit.

Again, Josh spoke with such confidence and had Scripture to go with everything he said. He talked about the Holy Spirit as a gift, and if we wanted this power of the Holy Spirit, all we had to do was ask for it.

"If a son asks for bread from any father among you, will he give him a stone? Or if he asks for a fish, will he give him a serpent instead of a fish? Or if he asks for an egg, will he offer him a scorpion? If you then being evil, know how to give good gifts to your children, how much more will your heavenly Father give the Holy Spirit to those who ask Him!" (Luke 11:11-13).

As we were leaving, Josh gave each of us a booklet to take home and read. It explained the baptism in the Holy Spirit in detail with Scripture. A few days later, I realized that Phil was reading the booklet. I was happy but surprised, because Phil only read the Sunday school lesson if he was asked to teach the youth class at church. He did not like to read, and I had never seen him sitting and reading before. As he read this information, he did not say a word. His face was so intent on what he was reading. He finished reading the booklet and started to read it again. He completed the second reading of it and then read it from the beginning a third time.

I did not say a word; I just let him read. Phil came to me and said, "Edna, if we do not get this baptism in the Holy Spirit, I am afraid we will be disobedient." As the words came out of his mouth so sincerely, I told him that maybe we should call Pastor Josh to see if he could help us. Phil walked over to the phone and called him and asked him if we could come over and talk with him about the baptism in the Holy Spirit.

We arrived at Josh's house, met his wife, and then the four of us sat at their kitchen table. Going through the Scriptures,

Josh started to explain the baptism in the Holy Spirit. As he read the Scriptures, I was realizing that I had a need for more of Christ and more of His Spirit living inside of me.

And being assembled together with them, He commanded them not to depart from Jerusalem, but to wait for the Promise of the Father, which, He said, "You have heard from Me; for John truly baptized with water, but you shell be baptized with the Holy Spirit not many days from now" (Acts 1:4-5).

When the Day of Pentecost had fully come, they were all with one accord in one place. And suddenly there came as a sound from heaven, as of a rushing might wind, and it filled the whole house where they were sitting. Then there appeared to them divided tongues, as of fire, and one sat upon each of them. And they were all filled with the Holy Spirit and began to speak with other tongues, as the Spirit gave them utterance (Acts 2:1-4).

Now when the apostles who were at Jerusalem heard that Samaria had received the word of God, they sent Peter and John to them, who, when they had come down, prayed for them that they might receive the Holy Spirit. For as yet He had fallen upon none of them. They had only been baptized in the name of the Lord Jesus. Then they laid hands on them, and they received the Holy Spirit (Acts 8:14-17).

While Peter was still speaking these words, the Holy Spirit fell upon all those who heard the word. And those of the circumcision who believed were astonished, as many as came with Peter, because the gift of the Holy Spirit had been poured out on the Gentiles also. For they heard them speak with tongues and magnify God (Acts 10:44-46).

And it happened, while Apollo's was at Corinth, that Paul having passed through the upper regions, came to Ephesus, and finding some disciples he said to them, "Did you receive the Holy Spirit when you believed?" So they said to him, "We have not so much as heard whether there is a Holy Spirit." And he said to them, "Into what then were you baptized?" So they said, "Into John's baptism." Then Paul said "John indeed baptized with a baptism of repentance, saying to the people that they should believe on Him who would come after him, that is, on Christ Jesus." When they heard this, they were baptized in the name of the Lord Jesus. And when Paul had laid hands on them, the Holy Spirit came upon them, and they spoke with tongues and prophesied (Acts 19: 1-6).

Josh read the scriptures to Phil and me as we sat there just soaking up the Word while the Spirit was drawing us to a new understanding of what all this meant. When I was young, I asked Jesus into my heart and got baptized in the Mennonite church because of fear of going to hell. Then, before witnessing at the Troy Fair, I had asked the Lord to forgive me because of sin in my life. I had a repentant heart and did not want sin in it, but I had never asked the Holy Spirit to come in and baptize me. I always thought that just automatically happened when I asked Jesus into my heart, but there was much more, and I wanted all of Christ I could have.

Since I had gone through depression and heard the audible voice of the Lord, I hungered for a relationship with Him. I wanted to be one with God like Deborah; I prayed that consistently. It was my heart's desire!

While we were in Josh's kitchen, he asked Phil and me to stand. We did, and then he asked us if we believed that if we asked for the Holy Spirit, God would give it to us. Just like Luke 11:11-13, we said, "Yes, we believe."

Josh prayed, and we repeated in a similar way people repent for salvation. We prayed that the Lord would fill us with His Holy Spirit. Josh instructed us to open our mouths and let the sound come out as his hand was on each of our heads. I could hear Josh praying in another language, and when I had asked for the Holy Spirit, something inside me started to rise up. It was like quivering inside but was not a physical thing. It was something I had never experienced before, and when Josh said, "Open your mouth," I believed by faith that the sounds coming out of my mouth were forming an unknown language. It was bubbling out of me like a spring that kept flowing. Phil was holding back a little bit, but he told me later that he was thinking too much. There was a language coming out of Phil that was not his own. It was his voice but not his language, because it was a heavenly language. It was language that is given only by the Holy Spirit.

CHAPTER 15

Restless

"Ask, and it will be given to you, seek, and you will find, knock, and it will be opened to you" (Matt. 6:33).

We had this joy inside of us like we knew there was something new, a new excitement, a new beginning. The next Sunday morning we went to church, and even though we knew that this was our church family and had been for the past eight years, we just felt like something was missing and did not understand it. When we got home from church, Phil and I both agreed that the next Sunday we would visit Victory Church where Josh pastored. God was starting to move us to the next season in our lives.

The next Sunday morning, we stepped into a little church that held eighty people, but there were 100 people there, so we crammed in. Friendly people greeted us, and everyone was excited and happy to be there. A sense of excitement was in the air. This was strange for us, because we always sat quietly on the bench at our church while waiting for the service to start. The people at this church were so excited as they talked and greeted one another. During the service, the worship was so alive. People clapped and raised their hands with excitement to sing to the Lord. The message was easy to understand, and I could tell by the look on Phil's face that he was understanding everything that was being said.

We heard a message explaining that we have a body with

a soul, and our soul is our mind, will, and emotions. We also have a spirit. Depending on the part we feed the most is what we will be, so if we feed our flesh the most and not the rest, we will be more flesh-minded. Or, if we measure most things by our feelings, most times our feelings do not measure up to what is actual truth. Or, we can feed our spirit man and stay in the Spirit. The Bible tells us to walk in the Spirit as He is in the Spirit (see Gal. 5:16). As we walk in the Spirit, the Holy Spirit teaches us, and we become more like Him and less of ourselves. This was just the beginning of a new life for us, and we would learn many things.

At the end of the service, people greeted us and extended an invitation for us to come back. A man and his wife approached our family and said to me, "I remember you. You were at the Troy Fair last summer. You were the one who was so fired up leading all those youth to Christ. You Mennonites surely get fired up."

Without even thinking, I said, "We do," although I was always taught not to be too emotional. He went on to say, "You remind me of Gerald Derstine. He was a Mennonite, too."

"I don't know this Gerald Derstine," I said. "I know Derstines, but I don't know Gerald."

He then suggested to me, "If you can ever get his book *Following the Fire*, read it . . . okay?

That morning, part of me felt like we should go back to our church family and tell them what happened, and then another part of me said that would not be a good idea. I missed our church family, but I wanted more of Jesus, too.

During this time, Kelsey and Kendra were going to New Covenant Christian School. I worked at the hospital, and Phil worked in construction ten to twelve hours a day with a one-hour drive to and from work. There was always so much to do on my day off, and I would often forget to eat lunch. By the time Phil would get home, my blood sugar would normally be low.

"You did not eat lunch again!" he would say. But on this one particular day off, I had decided to sit down and have a sandwich and turn on Sky Angel. My mom and Dad blessed us with a satellite and a full year of Sky Angel for our Christmas present. We were enjoying it, because there were so many speakers, singers, and kids' shows that were not bad.

While sitting on the recliner with my lunch on my lap, I flipped through the stations and came upon an older gentlemen preaching. I listened and liked him. He spoke simply, but had a lot to say. Halfway through his sermon, there was a break to tell about his book and the Christian retreat grounds he had up in Minnesota called Strawberry Lake Christian Retreat. The book, *Following the Fire* by Gerald Derstine, was what was advertised. I suddenly remembered a few weeks earlier when the man at church said I was like Gerald Derstine and that I should read his book. It was only $10, so I ordered it.

When Phil came home that night and I told him that this book was coming in the mail, he did not say much, although I was very excited to see what the book had to say. Phil had never read a book our whole married life, so I did not really expect him to read it, but I wanted to let him know how excited I was to read it. I told him all about this guy, Gerald and his sermon.

Kelsey and Kendra noticed a change in us after Phil and I had asked for the baptism in the Holy Spirit. They would often comment to us that we were different than we used to be. Our children watched us a lot, and children learn by example, so it is always good to think about what we say and do, because it affects our children.

Phil was reading the Scriptures just about every day, and he was taking notes at church every Sunday. When we would go to Victory Church, he would write down all the Scripture verses and then study them the next week. We had never seen him do this before; there was a definite change in him.

About the time we got filled with the Holy Spirit, we became so restless. We had already thought that we should sell our house, because we had so much debt. We owed Phil's parents money, and we had the mortgage on our house, car payments, and school tuition. But, this restlessness was different. It was something that I could not put my finger on; I just knew we had not ever felt this restless before. It was like an inner knowing that something was going to change our lives dramatically.

On Wednesday nights, we would go to prayer meeting at Victory Church. We had been going there regularly for about two months and were growing while seeking the Lord with this new hunger, so we surely did not want to miss any services. At the prayer meeting, Josh gave a short devotional and then the lights were turned down and the worship music was set on a low volume. We all spent time with the Lord however we sensed the Lord wanted us to pray and be with Him. Some walked around praying softly in the Spirit, while others knelt down at their benches just like we often did growing up in the Mennonite church. Some were just sitting, while others were writing, because they were receiving words from the Lord. As I knelt down to pray in the Spirit as the unknown language was coming out of my mouth, I sensed an urgency to share with the others in the prayer meeting to pray for Phil and me.

As we prayed one on one with the Lord for about twenty-five minutes, we then gathered and stood in a circle in the front of the church to collectively pray for any needs we had to share. This was always a powerful time. We saw miracles happen often during this time of prayer every week. To the group, I said, "Will you pray for Phil and me? I do not know what this restlessness is that we are both feeling lately; it makes no sense! We should not be restless at all." I shared that Phil had a good job with a good boss and that I was head of a department at the hospital, a job I loved. I stated that our girls were going to school and that we were in our dream home. "So, what is wrong with us?" I asked. As the group prayed, I sensed in my spirit we would have answers soon. People gathered around Phil and me with their hands on us, praying for an answer.

There was a new excitement in our home. The girls were asking many questions, and as their parents, we needed to be obedient to the Lord to give them the true answers. If we did not have it, we needed to find out what the Word said. Kelsey was thirteen, and seeing such a change in Phil and me, she would often say, "Daddy is so different."

One night at prayer meeting as we gathered in a circle in the front of the church, Kelsey asked if they would pray for her to receive the baptism in the Holy Spirit. As Josh laid hands on her, and as we all prayed in the Spirit, the presence of the Holy Spirit was very evident on Kelsey. She was weeping and shaking, but the Spirit-filled language was not coming out of her mouth. She was disappointed, because she wanted to have this heavenly language, too. We told her it was okay and that the Holy Spirit was still inside of her, but the language had not manifested itself as yet. "When this happens, we need to just thank Him for the gift of the Holy Spirit and keep believing that since we asked for the power of the Holy Spirit in our life, it is there," we explained.

A few days later, Kelsey came home from school just glowing. "Mom, Mom, during chapel today, we were singing worship songs, and as I was singing, another language started coming out, and I was singing in another language." The excitement she had was truly amazing; she knew that the presence of the Holy Spirit was real and living inside of her.

"I am so excited for you, Honey," I said. The joy in Kelsey's heart was bubbling over. There was so much we did not know and so much to learn about the presence of the Holy Spirit living inside of us, and the powers, strength, and comfort that only He can give. There was just so much to learn, and we were hungry. The more we learned, the more we wanted to learn.

CHAPTER 16

Depending on the Holy Spirit

Brethren, I do not count myself to have apprehended; but one thing I do, forgetting those things which are behind and reaching forward to those things which are ahead. I press toward the goal for the prize of the upward call of God in Christ Jesus (Phil. 3:13-14).

In the spirit realm, things started happening for me like never before. I know that may sound scary, but it really is not. Since we are a spirit with a body and a soul, if we choose to walk in the Spirit as He is in the Spirit, more of the supernatural things will happen. Sometimes, there just is not any explanation for them, so we must simply believe by faith that the Holy Spirit in us is at work, leading us to be all that He has called us to be for His honor and glory.

I was coming to the understanding that my life was way more than just being about me, my feelings, and desires. I was learning that it is about His Word and His thoughts and calling on our lives for His purpose, not ours. There was a time of dying to self that was Christ's gain. There was a renewal in my spirit that I had never known could exist, and the brightness of it was so hard to explain to the natural mind.

I reached a point where I knew in my spirit that I must depend on the power of the Holy Spirit to give me the strength I needed to keep my mind renewed according to His propose. I had been on 10 mg of depression medication, and there was a time when I was completely weaned off of it, but then another time when I thought I needed it to get through some stress, so I went back on it.   Now, I was realizing that if I believed with all my heart that Christ had given me His free gift not only for salvation but also for healing, then I was fully healed by His stripes. He paid that price for me, so I should receive that healing.

"Who Himself bore our sins in His own body on the tree, that we, having died to sins, might live for righteousness by whose stripes you where healed" (1 Peter 2:24).

I believed with all my heart that God would do that for me if I asked by faith, but I wanted to pray about this. Phil called Josh on the phone and explained to him how I was feeling and what I wanted. Josh asked to speak to me. "You believe that you are healed?" he asked once I got on the phone.

"Yes," I replied. When he prayed with me, I stopped taking the medication and never had a desire to take it again.

When I first went on the medication, it was a long process until the doctor found the best match for my body chemistry, but I had been on this particular one for almost five years now. When I first started taking the newer one, I felt clearer, as if a cloud had lifted, and everything seemed so much brighter. Now, in the power of the Holy Spirit, everything was even sharper and heightened in the things of the Spirit. This gave me a crystal clear picture of my soul's need. Because there was a keen sharpness with my spiritual sight, I could see things how God sees them so much more clearly.

Even though I did not understand or know about all the Holy Spirit could do through me, He was teaching me one step at a time. One day, while at work at the hospital, I checked my charts to see if we had any new patients. As I gathered my paperwork to interview the new patient, I was aware of the presence of the Holy Spirit with me. I knocked on the patient's door and introduced myself. The patient sat in her chair moving around restlessly with demon-like dark eyes. She glared at me and with a deep voice, she growled, "I know who you are! You came to kill me!"

I stared back into her demon eyes and did not look away. I felt love and compassion for her. She growled again, "You're going to kill me!"

"No, I am not here to kill you," I said. "I just want to ask you a few questions." My mind was on my job and the task at hand.

In a sweet voice, the patient then said, "Help me! Please help me!"

I began asking her questions from my interview sheet, but she did not respond to any of them, and I realized that there was no way I was going to get any information from her. As I turned to leave, a nurse who had been in the room the whole time, asked, "How can you look into her eyes like that? I can't stand to even look into her eyes."

"It does not bother me," I replied. At the end of the day when I gave the report to the head nurse, I told her the struggle I had with the patient and that I did not get very far with her.

"Well, that is because she has schizophrenia," she explained.

As I was driving home, I could not stop thinking about this woman. *Why did she think I was going to kill her, and why did her voice change so quickly?* I wondered. I suddenly remembered demons saying that to Jesus in the Bible. When demon-possessed people saw Jesus coming, they would say, "I know who you are!" Weeping, I prayed, "Lord, Lord, please forgive me! The demon that was in that woman knew the authority I had in You more than I did. Lord, I ask in Jesus' name that You would forgive me and please help me not to be so ignorant anymore to things of You." My heart went out to this poor woman who was trapped by this demon. That is why she said in a sweet voice, "Please help me; help me!"

"You believe that there is one God. You do well. Even the demons believe- and tremble!" (James 2:19).

A strength rose up inside of me that this demon must flee from this woman. I remembered hearing at church that there was no distance in the spirit realm, so I took authority over that demon and told it that it must leave and not come back. I told it in the power of Jesus Christ, it had no authority and it must leave that woman's body.

The next time I saw that dear woman, I invited her to a craft class. She was so sweet to me and stayed by my side while wanting me to sit beside her and help her. She was a dear lady and had peace about her this time that she did not have before. I believe with all my heart that the authority I have in Jesus Christ took care of that tormenting demon. Thank You, Jesus!

As a young child, I lived in fear all the time. During my depression, I was so fragile, and even before that, I would think I was the blame for everything. For me, saying "sorry" was a natural response to just about everything. It got to be so bad that at one point, a dear friend said to me, "Edna, just quit it! Quit being sorry for everything!" At that point, I realized just how much I said "sorry" because of my extreme lack of confidence and low self-esteem.

Since the Holy Spirit was manifesting in me so strongly, I now knew and understood the Word more clearly than ever. Plus, with this heavenly language, the Holy Spirit was revealing things to me as my Teacher and Comforter that I had not known and could not have known before.

I started getting a strong confidence in Christ with the Holy Spirit living in me that I could never have had in myself. The more the Holy Spirit revealed Himself in me, the more I knew who I was in Him. I did not need to have confidence in myself when the Holy Spirit gave me the confidence I needed to be who He wanted me to be. This was a freedom I had never known but had no idea how to explain to anyone what was happening. The Holy Spirit was teaching me and wanting me to learn from Him as He built me up in my faith before I would be able to explain it.

CHAPTER 17

Healing Power

"If you love Me, keep my commandments. And I will pray the father, and He will give you another Helper, that He may abide with you forever- the Spirit of truth, whom the world cannot receive, because it neither sees Him nor knows him; but you know Him, for He dwells with you and will be in you. I will not leave you orphans; I will come to you. A little while longer and the world will see Me no more, but I will see Me. Because I live, you will live also. At that day you will know that I am in My Father, and you in me, and I in you. He who has my commandments and keeps them, it is he who loves me. And he who loves Me will be loved by My Father and I will love him and manifest Myself to him" (John 14: 15-21).

A lot was happening in a short amount of time. The book I had ordered a few weeks earlier arrived. While reading it, I felt a connection with the author, Gerald Derstine. Because I grew up in the Mennonite church, I could relate to much of what he was saying. In his book, *Following the Fire*, he talked about growing up and that after he and his wife were married, God called them to the White Earth Indian Reservation in Northern Minnesota. While there, he was called to pastor the church that his uncle had started on the reservation as a missionary for the Native Americans.

While Gerald pastored Strawberry Lake Mennonite Church, he and his wife prayed with the youth of that church for revival in their area. The young pastor and the youth fasted and prayed earnestly for a year that God would bring revival to their small community of Strawberry Lake.

After a year of fasting and prayer, the Holy Spirit came in a way they had not expected in this little Mennonite church. People were falling out in the Spirit while speaking in other tongues and prophesying. Many young people came to the saving knowledge of Jesus Christ. The passion this man had to serve the Lord and to see revival was extraordinary. The heart he had for souls and leading people to Christ touched my spirit in a way I could not explain. I just knew that we had to get to this Gerald Derstine. I prayed earnestly that God would lead us to Gerald. "Lord, I ask in Jesus' name, please get us to Gerald Derstine. Father, in Jesus' name, please get Phil to Gerald. Lord, I don't care what You do, please help us to get to him," was my prayer.

As I continued reading this book, I learned that the Mennonite church had asked Gerald to leave, and he could no longer be part of that church. The Holy Spirit revealed to Gerald that the Mennonites did not understand, but they would in time. He believed this prophecy and believed that it would come true.

I finished the book and knew that Phil needed to read it, so I asked the Lord to give me the words to invite Phil to read this book that had touched me so much. Phil had been studying the Word, so maybe he would read a book, too. I went downstairs where Phil was sitting on the recliner. "Honey, I just finished this book by Gerald Derstine. It is a very good book, and I think you would like it and be able to relate to it, so I was wondering if you would read it?"

Phil agreed. I was excited. He started reading the book and finished it in three days. This was a very short time for him considering he spent about twelve hours a day at work and came home tired each day.

We had prayed at a Wednesday prayer meeting several weeks earlier about feeling restless. Phil and I talked about it, and we agreed that the first of the year we should fast and pray for twenty-one days for God's will in our lives. We had been hearing some preaching on fasting and knew this was what we needed to do. So, the Lord directed us to do a water fast for three days, and then we did a Daniel Fast for the remainder of the time. A Daniel Fast consists of eating only root foods, vegetables, beans, and nuts. During this fast, Kendra got very sick with high fevers that continued for at least ten days, and she would go in and out of being delirious, not knowing what she was doing.

One Wednesday night Kendra asked, "Mom, are we going to go to prayer meeting?"

"No, Honey, you are running such a high fever," I replied.

"But, Mom, I can't do this anymore. I have to go; I have to be anointed with oil," she exclaimed.

"Okay!" I said. I knew that we had to get there, because she needed some hope and healing. I had just taken her to the emergency room the night before, and the hospital staff told me that Kendra's sickness just had to run its course and to keep the fever down with medication.

That night when we arrived at church, I told Pastor Josh we could not stay, but Kendra wanted to be anointed with oil for healing. As Kendra walked to the front of the church with her sleeper and coat on, everyone gathered around her and started praying in the Spirit, and she was anointed with oil. This ten-year-old daughter of ours knew that Jesus was the only way she would get rid of her fever. By the time we put her to bed that night, she had no fever. We were praising the Lord! The next several days were long. Kendra did not have a fever anymore, but she was not well. I became very scared when she started coughing up blood clots. She was in and out of the hospital and seeing doctors several times during those twenty-one days of fasting. Phil told me with confidence, "This is an attack from Satan. He does not want us to fast and pray for God's will in our lives. We must continue!"

Our last day of the fast came, and Kendra awoke the very next day completely well, as if she never had been sick. She got through it with the covering and protection of the precious blood of Jesus. The restlessness that Phil and I had been experiencing for quite some time was now gone, and we had peace about what God wanted us to do. He was calling us to get rid of distractions in our life and the burden of debt. The Lord wanted us to sit at His feet with no distractions and just spend time with Him. We knew that the Institute of Ministry's ten-week course that Gerald Derstine hosted was what we must do.

The biggest distraction we had was money! We had put our house up for sale and believed it would sell. We knew that once it sold, God was calling us to go IOM (Institute of Ministry), a ten-week ministry training school at Strawberry Lake Christian Retreat. It was founded by Brother Gerald Derstine, and we knew that just spending time at Christ's feet was what the Holy Spirit was asking of us. Our plan was to attend the following summer after our house sold. There was also a training center and retreat grounds in Florida, but in my spirit, I knew we would be in Minnesota.

I was so drawn to the Strawberry Lake Christian Retreat that every week at work I would go on the Internet, since we did not have that at home, and look up the site and read about it over and over again, several times a week. I would tell everyone that we were going to Minnesota once our house sold.

CHAPTER 18

Faithful Stewards

"But seek ye first the kingdom of God and His righteousness, and all these things shall be added to you" (Matt. 6:33).

Early in my marriage, Phil and I struggled because of money. Phil was taught and believed he was the provider and did not and would not even think about asking God what He thought we should do with the money we had or needed. We thought that was not something you go to the Lord about. Boy, were we wrong! It is because of God that we had what we had in the first place. The money is all His, and how we use it can be a blessing or a curse.

Phil, changing all the time, was at a point where the Lord was speaking to him clearly about priorities with his time, money, and family. The Lord showed Matthew 6: 33-34 very clearly to Phil: "But seek first the kingdom of God and His righteousness, and all these things shall be added to you. Therefore do not worry about tomorrow, for tomorrow will worry about its own things. Sufficient for the day is its own trouble."

Phil got this verse in his spirit and started applying it to his life. He would not only read the Scriptures, but he would read the Bible first thing in the morning. He would set his clock for 5 every morning and read the Scriptures before he went to work. The very first week he started doing this, he noticed a difference. One day, he walked into the back door and came into the kitchen where I was making dinner, and said, "Honey, when I read first thing in the morning, my day goes better. I get more done and things just go better. It is like I have more time in the day than I used to!"

I could hear the excitement in his voice as he was telling me about this newfound wonder the Lord had shown him. It continued to amaze me how Scriptures that we had heard all our lives growing up all of a sudden made sense to the degree that we just wanted to be obedient and do what the Bible said. We knew if the Word said it, it must be true and would work.

Our pastor would often say, "B.I.B.L.E. Basic Instructions Before Leaving Earth." The hunger we both had for the Word was amazing. Phil took this even a step further and decided we should give the first of all our money we earned each week to the Lord. We had not been taught much about tithing in the Mennonite church and knew family members who did not think it was necessary to tithe. We heard things like, "You should take care of your own family before you give to the church." With the mentality that Phil was the head provider of our home and not God, I guess that would make sense to some people.

Phil and I did not see Phil as our main provider any longer. Instead, we saw God as our main provider, and we were just stewards of His blessings. With this mindset, it freed us up more than words can explain. The arguments about money and Phil getting quiet and building walls around himself when he looked at the checkbook would not be an issue as long as we looked at it from the right perspective. It was about God being in control of all areas of our livesnot just some parts, but everything. Phil stood on the Word and read it often to remind himself of the fact that God was our provider and the role we play as His children.

"Will a man rob God? Yet you have robbed Me! But you say, 'In what way have we robbed You?' In tithes and offerings. You are cursed with a curse, for you have robbed Me, even this whole nation. Bring all the tithes into the store house, that there may be food in My house, and try Me now in this, says the Lord of hosts, if I will not open for you the windows of heaven and pour out for you such blessings that there will not be room enough to receive it" (Mal. 3:8-10).

We started putting the first of every pay check in the offering plate, even when we were not sure how we would pay the bills. God said He would bless us, and we stood on that Word.

But this I say: He who sows sparingly will also reap sparingly, and he who sows bountifully will also reap bountifully. So let each one give as he purposes in his heart, not grudgingly or of necessity for God loves a cheerful giver. And God is able to make all grace abound toward you, that you, always having all sufficiency in all things, may have an abundance for every good work (2 Cor. 9:6-8).

"Give, and it will be given to you: good measure, pressed down, shaking together, and running over will be put into your bosom. For with the same measure that you use, it will be measured back to you" (Luke 6:38).

We decided that we would sow seeds and leave the harvest up to God, because it was all His anyway. Our faith was growing, and we knew our new, deeper-than-ever-before hunger and growing faith was from the Holy Spirit inside of us.. "Faith comes from hearing the word of God" (Rom. 10:17).

God was clearly showing us how He provides for His children when they obey Him. Soon after we started tithing, we found out that we were eligible for a partial tuition at the Christian school the girls had been attending. God is faithful and takes care of us. If He will take care of the sparrows of the field, how much more will He take care of us? (see Matt. 6:26)

CHAPTER 19

Changes

For this reason we also, since the day we heard it do not cease to pray for you, and to ask that you may be filled with all the knowledge of His will in all wisdom and spiritual understanding; that you may walk worthy of the Lord, fully pleasing Him, being fruitful in every good work and increasing in the knowledge of God; strengthened with all might, according to His glorious power, for all patience and longsuffering with joy; giving thanks to the Father who has qualified us to be partakers of the inheritance of the saints in the light. He has delivered us from the power of darkness and conveyed us into the Kingdom of the Son of His love (Col. 1:9-13).

Things were changing in our personal lives, our family, and in our marriage. We were communicating better than ever, and we reached a point where I loved to spend time with Phil again. There was a time when I was going through the depression and believing lies from Satan that I did not know if Phil loved me or if he ever really did. I did not know if I really loved him all that much, either, (but when you get married, it is for life). It was like going through the motions with me battling depression and him focusing on the money more than anything or anyone else. We were a sad pair for several years, and now it had been almost five years since that all took place.

It was a beautiful day. Phil and I were driving to Walmart while the girls were in school. Phil had the day off, and that was rare for us to have time together in the middle of the week. Phil was getting ready to go on a mission's trip to Louisiana. I had told Phil soon after our fast that I had a desire to do missions. I reminded him about when we were dating and he told me that someday we would do missions together. He was not experiencing a similar desire as mine to pursue missions, but he knew he was supposed to go along on a mission's trip to Louisiana to help build houses that were damaged from Hurricane Katrina.

As we were driving to Walmart, we talked about the upcoming trip and all that was going on. I silently asked God, "Lord, why did Phil and I have to go through all that in our marriage five years ago? Why did our marriage almost fail?" As soon as I said it, I just let it go and then started talking to Phil about what we needed to get at the store.

While we were shopping, Phil said, "Honey, I need to go to the bathroom. I will be right back." I waited by the cash register since we had already gotten our things. While waiting, I heard the Holy Spirit say, "I have great plans for you and Phil in the ministry. That is why Satan wanted you apart." Phil walked out of the bathroom at that time. I was so overwhelmed by the clarity and precise answer I had just clearly heard as if someone standing right beside me had just said it.

The next Saturday morning as Phil was getting ready for his trip, he said, "Honey, I know I am supposed to go on the mission's trip. I am not sure why, but I know I must go. I will need you to pray for me, because it is going to be hard for me to go when I know we are going to be short with cash this week."

"What do you mean we are going to be short?" I asked with a puzzled look on my face.

"I was sure we had enough in the checking account to pay the bills for this week, but when I looked at the checkbook, I realized we are going to be $350 short," He explained. He had such a concerned look on his face as he continued to talk, "Pray for me so that I can go, knowing we need the money."

"I will pray, and God is going to work it all out," I assured him with a smile. I had no idea how this was going to work, but if Phil felt he was to go, then I wanted him to go. It was funny to me, though, because I was the one who had a heart for missions, yet he was the one going on the missions trip.

The next day at church, Kelsey, Kendra, and I walked in together without Phil. It seemed odd to not have my husband with us. The message spoke to me very much that day, and I had tears in my eyes at the end of the service when one of the men from church stopped me in the aisle and said, "Edna, I probably should have told you this before service, but the Lord spoke to me and told me that He had great plans for you and Phil in the ministry together doing missions, and I am suppose to help support you financially. Is there anything at all I can help you with?"

I could not believe what I was hearing. As the tears were running down my cheeks along with the memories of just recently having heard something very similar in the Walmart, I was overwhelmed. Before I could even think of the magnitude of all that was happening, I just said, "$350."

He replied without any hesitation and a smile on his face, "I will bring it over tomorrow."

Phil came home from his mission's trip the next week with a brand new desire for missions that was not present when he initially left for the trip. With a smile on his face, he said, "I was helping this woman fix up her house, doing the same work I do every day in construction, and she could not believe I would come all this way to fix up her house. I want to be able to help others with the skills that I have. This woman, with tears in her eyes, could not believe someone would do that for her." Phil was meant to go on that trip so he would know that God was calling us to do mission's work. God is so good, and He just loves setting us up!

CHAPTER 20

The Faith of a Child

"Let the little children come to Me, and do not forbid them; for of such is the kingdom of God. Assuredly, I say to you, whoever does not receive the kingdom of God as a little child will by no means enter it" (Mark 10:14-15).

The spiritual growth of our children was happening as well. They were watching our faith grow and often telling us that we were not the same as we once were. Kendra had always been a very active girl and needed to be doing several things at one time. She liked to keep moving, and with so much energy, a good way to help with that was by keeping her active. She was very good at soccer, so that was a good way for her to stay active. She suffered from asthma so badly, though, that she needed to use her inhaler before a soccer game and then again at half-time and at the end. It helped her breath, so she could run without having a problem breathing.

Kendra did not always go with us to Wednesday night prayer at Victory Church. She needed time for healing from the high fever she had when we were fasting. Normally, she would go to the Mennonite church on Wednesday nights for the Kids Club and to be with her friends she knew since she was very small. But this one Wednesday evening, Kendra said, "Mom, I want to go to prayer meeting tonight."

I was surprised, so I asked, "Are you sure you want to go?"

"Yes!" she exclaimed. The persistence in her voice let me know I was not going to talk her out of it.

"Okay, you can go, but you must be respectful while others are praying and not distract me or anyone else during prayer time." I knew that sitting there while we had our one-on-one prayer time with the Lord might be a little much for her. But she promised that she would be good. The faith of a child!

At prayer meeting, and during the time of prayer, Kendra just sat there like she was waiting for something. I was praying in the Spirit on my knees, and every once in a while looked over at her, and she was just sitting there waiting. I wondered what was going through that little eleven-year-old girl's head. As we gathered at the front of the church to lift up each other in prayer, Kendra pulled on my arm, and with a very anxious voice, said, "Mom, Mom, ask Pastor Josh if he will anoint me with oil so I won't have asthma anymore."

"Okay, Honey!" I said while witnessing the urgency in her face and voice. "Josh, Kendra's wondering if you would anoint her with oil tonight for healing of her asthma?"

Josh, a man well over six feet tall, bent down in front of Kendra and asked, "Kendra, do you understand what you are asking for? By asking to be anointed with oil, you are believing that God can heal you of asthma?"

Kendra shook her little head and said, "I know!"

"Do you believe it?" Josh asked,

"Yes." Kendra answered with confidence in her voice.

She was anointed with oil that night, and the very next morning we could tell she had been healed. She was not coughing and she never had to use an inhaler again for soccer or anything else. A few months later, she got a bad cold, and the doctor wanted her to be retested for asthma on a machine at the hospital. She had taken this test before but could not continue it because of her asthma. The respiratory therapist could not even induce asthma to the highest point, because Kendra's asthma had been so bad. This time, however, when she took the test, the respiratory therapist set the levels as high as possible, and it never affected Kendra. She no longer had asthma, even with a cold, because God healed her completely, and she is still healed today.

Kendra's faith and her strong desire for God to heal her was encouragement to me. The Holy Spirit revealed to her spirit that she was to be healed the night at the prayer meeting, and there was no doubt in Kendra's mind about that. "Faith of a little child shall lead them" (Isa. 11:6). Because of the faith that Kendra revealed, others from church also received healing after Kendra's healing experience with God. God is so good, and by His stripes we are healed.

My Soul Longed for You

 Intercession

But you beloved, building yourself up on your most holy faith, praying in the Holy Spirit (Jude 1:20).

As I continued to grow in the Spirit, the gifts were being manifested, and the Holy Spirit was showing me things. He is the great Teacher. There are times when heaviness would fall upon me, and I knew that the Holy Spirit was wanting me to pray in the Spirit for someone or something. During those times, often I would have a vision, or I would just keep praying in tongues until I broke through and felt peace.

When this first started happening, I did not know what to think, and I did not even know it was called "praying in the Spirit," because I was taught that if you speak in tongues, you must interpret it or else it is a sin. Then, Phil was taught that speaking in tongues was of the devil, so we had a lot to learn.

One night as I was dreaming, it was like I was watching someone who was about to overdose on drugs. I could see very clearly as I watched this person take the drug and a razor blade and chop up the drug and then make a straight line with the powder they were about to sniff. Next, I felt a tap on my shoulder. It could not have been Phil, because he was sound asleep on the other side of me. Immediately I knew I must pray, because what I was seeing in my dream was actually a vision of someone ready to sniff that drug. I prayed in the Spirit for as long as it took. I knew when it was over and everything was okay, because I felt a peace come over me, and I knew the Holy Spirit intervened.

This is called *intersession*, and it is very humbling for me to have a gift as such. God, in all His mercy, was letting me know a few years earlier at Black Rock Women's Retreat that I did not have any idea what that word *intercession* was or what it meant. I had never heard of it. In fact, I had never heard of anyone ever having things like this happen to them, and I was not sure I should say anything about my experiences to anyone. But over the years, God put people around me who helped me, and when I was mentored by a sweet older woman on the gift of intersession, the gift became even stronger. It was not what she said that taught me. Rather, it was how she demonstrated her gift while I was with her that brought the gift out in me. I had come to a greater understanding of how important it is as believers who have the power of the Holy Spirit in their lives to stand in the gap for our nation, for others in need or emergency situations.

Praying in the Spirit is so important, and we do not always know what to say, but the Spirit of God living in us does. When speaking that heavenly language, the Spirit is speaking through me and you in those moments.

> *Likewise, the Spirit also helps in our weakness. For we do not know what we should pray for as we ought, but the Spirit Himself makes intercession for us with groaning which cannot be uttered. Now He who searches the hearts knows what the mind of the Spirit is, because He makes intercession for the saints according to the will of God.*

Then it goes on to say:

> *And we know that all things work together for good to those who love God to those who are the called according to His purpose (Rom. 8:26-28).*

I have heard that last verse spoken in church my whole life, but I have come to a new understanding that verses 26 and 27 go right along with it. This is why all things work together for good to those who love the Lord, because the Holy Spirit is interceding on behalf of any and all situations of the people who love the Lord.

There have been many times when something has happened at church, in the family, or with friends that I had no idea of what to pray. When you are asked to pray for a situation and you are at a loss for words, remember the Holy Spirit knows, and if we just humble ourselves by faith and pray in the Spirit, God will intervene on what is best to pray.

For he who speaks in a tongue does not speak to men but to God, for no one understands him; however in the spirit he speaks mysteries (1 Cor. 14:2).

As my Teacher, the Holy Spirit has shown me that when my faith is weak, I should come to Him, and He will encourage me. My love language is full of words of affirmation and encouragement that speak volumes to me. When I am praying in tongues and am in the Spirit, I sense encouragement, peace, and confidence that not even an encouraging word from someone else could match.

But you beloved, building yourself up on your most holy faith, praying in the Holy Spirit (Jude 1:20).

When I am in the Spirit, I can pray, speak, know the thoughts of the Holy Spirit, and sing in the Spirit. What is the conclusion then? "I will pray with the Spirit, and I will also pray with the understanding. I will also sing with the understanding." (1 Cor. 14:15).

I have always heard that when I accepted Jesus as my

Savior, the Holy Spirit came to live in me and be my Teacher. While growing up, it was such a chore reading the Scriptures, because I could not understand what I was reading. However, once I received the power of the Holy Spirit by faith, He in His wisdom showed me things I never knew before.

When I accepted Jesus Christ as my Savior, I received eternal life. I initially thought that I was just supposed to wait around until I died. Not knowing what to do in the meantime was my problem. Now, however, I had a new understanding of the Holy Spirit, and I needed to walk by faith and use the gift of tongues to grow in Him to a fuller understanding of what He had called me to do.

CHAPTER 22

Learning to Trust

Trust in the Lord with all your heart, and lean not on your own understanding; In all your ways acknowledge Him, and he shall direct your path (Pro. 3: 5-6).

We spoke with a neighbor about buying our house, and he said he would. This would happen just in time for us to go to Minnesota for the ten-week ministry training. Phil and I had planned on a date that I would hand in my letter of resignation to the hospital where I worked, and we were going through all our belongings and giving things away. We also had a big moving sale as we prepared to go. The night before I was planning on handing in my resignation to the hospital, the man who was planning to buy our house contacted us to let us know he was backing out because of some kind of family issue.

Phil and I were out in the garage when I said to Phil, "I have my letter ready and was planning to submit it tomorrow, but now we don't have a buyer for the house."

With a look of determination, Phil said, "Hand in your letter tomorrow the way we planned. Moses told the Israelites they should move forward, and we are going to move forward, too." There had been times over the past several years that I had seen that same look on Phil's face. During those times, when he was not speaking from his head, I knew that God was working through him, especially when it made no sense to the natural mind.

The next morning, I handed my letter to my boss at the hospital, and she received it so graciously. She was always very nice to me and was intrigued by my faith. She would tell me that she appreciated how I spoke so positively about things. This was a huge compliment, because years back, I was not a positive person. I used to see everything as 100 percent worse than it really was. Now that I was believing the truth, and knowing what the truth actually was, my outlook was a whole lot brighter. Not living in fear and believing the lies of the Enemy made my attitude more positive. My boss let me know that if I ever wanted my job back, it would be open for me. The favor of the Lord was on us many times throughout this process.

One Sunday morning as Phil was in the bathroom shaving, I turned on the television to watch one of our favorite preachers, and he was preaching on favor. He was saying that there was a right time, place, and people who will come in your life if you follow the Lord's leading. As he preached, the Holy Spirit came upon me, and I started to weep to the point I could not talk. "Mommy, Mommy, what is wrong?" Kelsey asked. Then, she ran up the stairs, and I could hear her say, "Daddy, Daddy, come quickly! Something is wrong with Mommy."

Phil quickly came down the steps with no shirt on and partially shaven. "Honey, what is wrong?" he asked.

I finally managed to get out of my mouth, "Phil, we must pray right now that God would lead us to the right people at the right time and in the right place!" I knew that this was crucial to our future to have the favor of God on us and to ask Him to direct our steps in this way.

He sat down next to me, took my hands, and prayed that the Lord would lead us and give us favor to have the right people come into our lives at the right time and places. Peace came over me, and I knew it was complete. I thanked the Lord for what He was going to do. The very next week at church, one of the women came up to me and said, "Edna, I ordered you a book that should be here in a week or so. It is called *Right People, Right Place, Right Plan.* I just felt you should have it." This was a confirmation. We have had so many divine appointments over the years and supernatural things at the right places and the right times. God is faithful.

After I gave my two-week's notice at work, I was a full-time stay-at-home mom, and I loved it. I had never been home full time. I had worked our whole marriage, because making sure that there was enough money in the checkbook was the most important thing. Now that we had given our life completely to the Lord, had surrendered, and was praying that the Lord would take full control of our lives through the leading of the Holy Spirit, what the checkbook said was not always the truth of what we had in Him.

I loved that summer. Our house did not sell, so I got to spend the whole summer at home with Kelsey and Kendra without having to leave for work or dragging them along to work with me. We enjoyed spending time outside on our 32 acres. It was funny that now that we were selling our home, we were enjoying it more.

Even though I enjoyed the summer very much, I was wondering if I could hear the voice of God as clearly as I had at times. I had believed for several months that we would be going to Strawberry Lake Christian Retreat in Minnesota. I was so sure we were going there for the ten-week ministry training. I had told everyone that when I left my job that we would be heading to Minnesota. But when our house did not sell in time for us to go, I did not understand why things weren't falling into place as I strongly believed they would.

However, during that summer, our faith grew so much. Faith comes from hearing and by hearing the Word of God. We often spoke out the Word over and over to the situations at hand. I was not working, but we still had the same amount of bills coming in every week. Some friends of ours came over to pray with us one night and encouraged us to take authority over the checkbook that Satan had no right to. As we sat around the dining room table with our friends, Phil put the checkbook in the middle of the table, and he and I put our hands on it. Our friends put their hands on top of ours, and we declared and let Satan know he had no authority in our lives and our finances. Then we prayed protection over us and all that the Lord had given us and that He would provide.

God worked! There would be times when, according to the checkbook, it did not look like there would be enough to pay the bills that month, but thanks to God and His glory, all the bills got paid. We continued faithfully to give the first portion of Phil's paycheck to the Lord every week. It was all God's anyway, and we had surrendered it to Him. He is our provider, not us, and He proved Himself to us.

CHAPTER 23

Water Baptism

But without faith it is impossible to please Him, for he who comes to God must believe that He is, and that He is a rewarder of those who diligently seek him. By faith Abraham . . . obeyed; when he was called to go out to the place which he would receive as an inheritance obeyed; and he went out, not knowing where he was going (Heb. 11:6, 8).

Our house sold a week before Christmas in 2007. We had just a few things left that we put in a 10 x 10 storage shed, not knowing when we would be back for those belongings. We had given or sold most everything away that we owned and had no debt. We were ready to sit at Christ's feet with no distractions. We arrived at Florida Christian Retreat the second week of January to start the ten-week ministry training. The excitement in our spirit was like none we had ever known before. People thought we were crazy. Others admired us. Then, there were others who just did not know what to think, but that did not matter to us. We were ready, and when God called, we knew we had to go.

I was homeschooling the girls in Florida. I would tell them their assignments, and they would do them while Phil and I were in class. If they had any questions, they would skip over them, and we would go over them together on Mondays. Monday was our day off, so that's when Phil and I would sit with the girls and go over questions, do grading, and go over assignments for the next week. It still blows my mind how we homeschooled, plus we went to ten weeks of ministry training, 300 hours of intense ministry training. All I know is our God is a God of increase, and if He says to do it, He will make a way.

We were experiencing things we never seen before. It was not easy getting to class at 8 in the morning and going until 3 p.m. and then going back at 7 p.m. until whenever the Holy Spirit said the evening service was over. We got tired in the flesh, but our spirit-man was renewed, and God was working on my soul. I felt as if I was an onion being peeled, and everything that God could not use for His honor and glory was exposed and thrown away. Then God started working on filling me up with what He had for me.

Phil and I learned a lot in the Spirit realm and also about each other and what would block us from moving forward in Him to fulfill the call in our lives. We got rid of a lot that was from the past.

During one of our morning sessions, the assistant pastor said that there would be a baptism in the Manatee River that afternoon for anyone who wanted to be baptized. As Phil and I discussed it, we had decided that we wanted to be baptized and not for salvation but rather for putting the past behind and moving forward to all that God had for us in our future with Him.

As we got down to the river, there were people gathered along the shore, and the assistant pastor was there baptizing people. Kelsey and Kendra came with us and wanted to watch Mom and Dad be baptized. As we stepped into the Manatee River, the pastor said to Phil and me, "I want to baptize you together at the same time," so he got another man to help so we could go under the water together and come back up together. Phil had only been sprinkled in the Mennonite church when he got baptized, so this was a new experience for him.

The pastor looked at us with intensity in his face and said, "The Holy Spirit wants me to anoint you with oil before you go under the water. I don't know why," he said, but he knew he must be obedient to the leading of the Holy Spirit. I knew right away why the Holy Spirit wanted to have us anointed with oil. It was for healing from the past. Phil and I had decided that we were going to leave all generational curses over our lives and our children at the bottom of the Manatee River, along with relationships that came between Phil and me, Christ and us, and bad choices we had made for our family and each other. This was also a time of healing and not just moving forward.

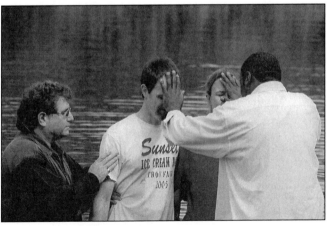

Phil and Edna receiving the oil on their head just before baptism.

The pastor anointed us with oil on our foreheads, and then he and another man took Phil and me, and we went down under the water at the same time. When we came up at the same time, the power of the Holy Spirit was so strong and the presence of the Lord so great that people were falling over on the shore. Phil was shaking uncontrollably, and the gift of tongues were just bubbling out of me like a fountain.

The pastor started prophesying. His huge, brown eyes looked at us so intensely, and I knew God was working. He was working on getting something very important into mine and Phil's spirits. As we stood there shaking in the Spirit, the pastor said, "Phil and Edna, read the Word! Read the Word! Read the Word! Know the Greek and the Hebrew of the Word. Know the Word! You will be under several different ministries, and then you will have your own ministry."

I could not take my eyes off of this intense look on the pastor's face, an intensity that communicated that we must get this, that we must get it into our spirit. Phil was still shaking in the Spirit about half an hour later. The girls met us at the bank of the river as we walked out onto dry land. "Dad, Mom, did you see that? Did you see the people falling over on the bank when you and Daddy came up out of the water? Why were they falling?" The questions were rapidly coming out of the girls' mouths, and they had looks of amazement on their sweet faces.

"When the presence of the Holy Spirit is so strong, you fall over sometimes, because the weight of His glory is so wonderful," I said.

CHAPTER 24

School of the Spirit

And it shall come to pass in the last days, says God, that I will pour out of My Spirit on all flesh; your sons and you daughters shall prophesy, your young men shall see visions, your old men shall dream dreams, and on My menservants and on My maidservants I will pour out My Spirit in those days; and they shall prophesy (Acts 2:17-18).

The Lord often speaks to me in dreams, and I had many during this time. One night, I had a dream that I was a beautiful bride. I had a long, white beautiful gown on, and my hair was perfect. As I was waking up, I could hear very clearly the Lord telling me in my spirit, "Edna, you are my beautiful bride." From that point on, I had decided that when I would go to the evening services, I would try to look my best. I thought about how often in my life I wanted to look good so other people would think I looked good. Now it was time for me to want to look good for my Abba Father.

Many supernatural things happened during this ten weeks; it was a school of the Spirit, so the Spirit was very present with us the whole time. One evening as a prophetic worship was happening in the tabernacle, people would just come in and soak up His presence and go before Him in worship. People were on the floor faced down, raising their hands. Some were sitting and just meditating on His goodness. There were many different acts of worship present in the room that evening. Phil, the girls, and I were sitting in our seats just soaking up the heavenly worship when we realized that there was a sound like a mighty wind, and the air was blowing, and we could feel it as our hair was blowing. Phil looked at me, and I looked at him. He said with his face just glowing from being amidst it all, "Do you feel that wind?"

In total amazement, I responded, "This is just like what happened in the Book of Acts!" The power and the presence of the Holy Spirit is so real so often, but when you have never experienced the supernatural work of the Holy Spirit, the rush you get is like nothing that can be explained.

Another time when sleeping, I would wake up and hear the Holy Spirit say, "Be still and know that I am God!" (Ps. 46:10). I would then fall back asleep and wake up a few hours later and hear, "Be still and know that I am God." Then again a few hours later, I would wake up and hear, "Be still and know that I am God." For the next couple of days, those words were ringing in my head over and over again, "Be still and know that I am God!"

Our whole family was blessed. Kelsey and Kendra had been told by the doctors that they had scoliosis and that their spines were crooked. There was a speaker at our training who was laying hands on people, and they were being healed. Kelsey and Kendra went forward for healing that their spines would be straight. We had previously-taken X-rays with us and had been advised to find a doctor when we got settled. As the speaker laid hands on the girls and prayed, one of their legs got longer. Kelsey said she could feel a considerable difference, and she saw her leg grow out. Praise the Lord! The girls were running around all over the retreat grounds telling everyone God healed them. There was an excitement that was in the air!

One night, I had a dream about my dad. In the dream, he did not want me to go out a door and tried to stop me from going. This dream disturbed me, and I told our dean about it. I shared this concern of mine with Brother Gerald Derstine and said that I did not think that either of our parents wanted us to be there. Both parents were asking a lot of questions before we left Pennsylvania and did not necessarily think we should go to the Christian retreat for ministry training. Anything we had heard about Brother Gerald up to this point was that he was radical, and so neither of the parents were too excited about us going to ministry training. They reminded us that there were other Mennonite Bible schools that we could go to if we wanted to go to school. When I told Gerald about this, he said, "Edna, do you mind if I call your dad?"

"No, I don't care," I said. I had no idea what Gerald was going to say to him, and I never heard what he said, but it must have been a turning point.

Dad called me a few days later and said, "Edna, Mom and I are coming down to Florida to come to your graduation. After the ten weeks of intensive ministry training, there was a banquet and a graduation held for the students. This school was different, because it was not all about studying. Since it was a school of the Spirit, whatever God spoke to the teacher at that moment in his or ministry calling is what they portrayed and spoke into our lives. The teachers were anyone from pastors, missionaries, street ministers, healing ministers, prophets, and teachers who were all being used of God and serving Him by speaking into our lives and sharing the Holy Spirit with us.

When my mom and dad arrived at the retreat, they were so amazed at their driving time. They had arrived a day earlier than planned and did not understand how that could have happened. I just suspected that God had a reason, because God is a God of His timing! That night, there was a prophet who was speaking. I was not sure how Mom and Dad would like him. I knew this speaker would be speaking out prophecies and that we would see signs and wonders. I did not know if they had ever seen this before.

Dad and Mom sat in the very back row of the auditorium. IOM students were required to sit in the front row of the tabernacle that holds several hundred people. During the service, as the prophet was preaching, he did not stand in one place. He would go back and forth, and every once in a while, he would just break out in tongues and then interpret to us what was being said.

Toward the end, this prophet had us all hold hands across the aisles. I heard the Holy Spirit say, "Edna, go get your dad!" I went to the aisle and took hold of the people's hands that were blocking the aisle, and said, "Excuse me! Excuse me! Excuse me!" while moving all the way up the aisle and breaking people's hands apart until I got to the very back row where my dad stood. His eyes where wide with amazement, and I said, "Dad, come with me!" I did not give him an option, and he followed so obediently that it shocked me. But, when we turned to go back down the aisle to the front of the tabernacle, everyone had their hands together again, so I had to use the same system I had used getting to my dad. As Dad and I were standing there in the front row, the prophet spoke vibrantly while going back and forth across the front of the room. We stood there for a few minutes, and I began wondering, *Why in the world did I just go get my dad?*

I started to question if maybe I had heard the Holy Spirit wrong, but then, all of a sudden, the speaker was standing in front of my dad and said, "You are being healed of sugar diabetes. Blood disorder be gone! You think because your grandfather died early and your father died early that you will die early, but you will not die. You will go back to be a testimony."

I stood by my dad's side weeping, tears running down my face, because ever since I could remember, I knew that he had said that he was going to die young because his father and grandfather had. I knew he had suffered with blood sugar problems for many years. Just a few weeks before my parents came to Florida, Dad had called and said that he had a rare blood disorder. He stood in front of this prophet with not a word to say. His eyes were glazed over, and he looked like he was in shock.

After the service, Dad and I went up to the speaker, and Dad said to the prophet, "I think I am a little bit of a doubting Thomas."

The prophet replied with authority, "Watch your confession! It is so important to not say a negative word after you have received a healing, so you do not get it back. We must speak life over ourselves, not death or curses. As my dad started to walk away, and I turned to walk away, the speaker looked into my eyes and said, "Edna, God did that for you."

The next night at the banquet before the graduation, my dad said to me with honor in his voice, "Edna, I am proud of you." God has blessed my relationship with my dad. The fear I had as a child, along with the hurt and bitterness has all gone, and I am thankful for the love of Jesus and His cleansing power to wash all the pain away. I love my dad and know without a shadow of a doubt, that I was meant to be his daughter. We have a relationship like never before. We talk on the phone about spiritual things. He will often say, "Edna, I had a dream. What does this mean?" Recently, he said to me on the phone, "I am not feeling well. Will you say one of your magic prayers for me?"

I laughed, and said, "Yes, Dad. I will." It is not magic but the precious blood of Jesus and the power of the Holy Spirit living inside of me that makes my dad want me to pray for him. God is faithful!

CHAPTER 25

Visions

"A little while longer and the world will see Me no more, but you will see Me. Because I live, you will live also. At that day you will know that I am in My Father, and you in Me, and I in you. He who has My commandments and keeps them, it is he who loves Me. And he who loves Me will be loved by My Father, and I will love him and manifest Myself to him" (John 14:19-21).

Phil and I were sitting in class listening to a speaker who had the gift of prophetic worship, so she was speaking for several days on worship. She was explaining that when you get in the presence of the Lord to worship, it is like you need to go through the eye of a needle and leave all your gifts, talents, relationships, and any part of you that may hold you back from worshiping. She was saying that we have to let it go and come through the eye of the needle to the other side, just you and God to worship Him.

I wanted that more than anything, because my heart's desire was, is and always will be to be one with Abba Father, Jesus Christ, the Holy Spirit. To be one with God, like Deborah. I prayed, "Lord Jesus, I want to come through the eye of the needle to worship You. I leave all my gifts, talents, Phil, Kelsey, Kendra, and all relationships on the other side, and I come through to worship You." At the end of this prophet's teaching, she said God had given her a song, and she asked us to close our eyes and just let the Holy Spirit speak to us.

As I was sitting there with eyes shut, I was not really thinking of anything. I was simply listening to the beautiful music, and all of a sudden I had a vision of my time back in the psychiatric ward. I saw myself in the hospital room sitting up in bed, and the lights from the helicopter were coming in the window while I was shaking and hearing the audible voice of the Lord say, "No, you do not have a relationship with Me!" As I was seeing this vision so clearly and hearing the music in the room, I felt in my spirit what God feels when He does not have a relationship with us. He loves us so much and just wants to be with us, but we put these limits on Him because of selfishness, fear, other relationships, or even religion. There are so many things that can block us from having a relationship with Him instead of being free in Him and knowing that we are one.

As I was sitting there and crying so hard in travail and shaking and weeping, others in the class had no idea what was so wrong. I could not speak the anguish He feels when we do not have Him in control of our lives , and the pain He feels when other things, people or priorities, take over. He is waiting and longing for a relationship with each one of us. He is longing for His pure spotless bride. He loves us so much that He sent His own Son to die on the cross for our sins. That is the most amazing love, and His heart aches for us.

I sat there weeping for at least thirty minutes. Phil had no idea what was going on. He sat there rubbing my back, and people were gathering around me praying and speaking words of encouragement. The prophet-speaker sensed in her spirit that it was rejection! I was crying so hard that I could not tell them that it was not my rejection, but that I was feeling it was God's rejection when we do not have a relationship with Him.

That afternoon I did not go to class. Instead, I spent time in my room praying and being alone with my Abba Father. I could not be with anyone else. I just needed to be with my Daddy. Praying in the Spirit and being with Him in the Spirit, as He is Spirit. I wondered what all that was about that had just happened with me, but God was working on my heart so clearly for His purpose.

The next week, while at Gerald and Beulah's house for shoe-fly pie, we were asked what God had been showing us so far in our IOM class. The students shared what the Lord was speaking to them and what they were learning. Phil and I were sitting at the very end of all the students, so I would be the last one to speak. The closer it got to being my turn, the more I knew that the Holy Spirit wanted me to give my testimony about what had happened the week before in class. My heart was racing, and I was shaking. I felt like if I did not share, I would explode.

I was very honest and told them of my past of being in the psychiatric hospital, having depression, not having any self-worth, being suicidal, and how the Lord spoke to me in an audible voice. I shared how the week before, God allowed me to feel what He felt when I rejected Him. As we were leaving the Derstine's home that day, Brother Gerald said, "Thank you so much for sharing with us."

"You're welcome, but I have no idea why God wanted me to share that."

That evening, as we were in service, the worship was so powerful, and I had just told the Lord the week before that I would come through the eye of the needle to worship Him alone, without anything or anybody, just Him and me. As I was standing there worshiping Him with all thoughts toward Him, singing with all my might, hands raised, the Holy Spirit took me in a vision back to that room in the psychiatric ward with me sitting there in the bed and the helicopter lights going around. This time, instead of hearing the Lord's voice telling me, "You don't have a relationship with Me," I saw Jesus standing in my room with His arms opened wide to me as He came to me and held me. At that moment, I felt the most amazing love that I had never felt before. I knew who my Daddy, Abba Father was, and I knew He loved me! The vision lasted just for a few moments, but the experience, the love, and the power of it will last in my heart forever.

After we finished our ten weeks at IOM, we were asked by Brother Gerald Derstine if we would come to Strawberry Lake Christian Retreat in Minnesota. We served there for four years on staff and were blessed mightily with many supernatural blessings. On Valentine's Day 2009, God woke me up in the middle of the night. As I was praising Him as I often do in the night, I said, "Lord, I love You! I praise You! I thank You for being my God, my Father, my all and all." I heard my Daddy, Abba Father speak again: "You are my Deborah!"

* * *

Amazing Love! How could it be that You should die for me? His love truly is amazing, and He just wants to show each of us, by having a relationship with us, how much He does love us! Won't you receive His love and accept Him as Lord of your life today?

I pray that in Jesus' name that everyone who reads this story will clearly see how Jesus Christ worked in my life to show me how much He loves me and wants me to have a relationship with Him. My story of tragedy, pain, and fear led me to finding out who I am in Christ, and His amazing love shows who Christ is in me. May you also know who you are in Him and who He is in you!

I pray that this story will bless each reader, and that the presence of the Holy Spirit would be evident in each one of you as you seek His face. God's mercy and grace abounds to each of us as we move forward in seeking Him for a relationship that is just between you and Him. The great thing about it is that He is intimate with each one of us in a special way. He loves each one of us so much!

Phil and Edna Cassel